Consul Willshire Butterfield

History of the Discovery of the Northwest by John Nicolet in

1634

With a Sketch of His Life

Consul Willshire Butterfield

History of the Discovery of the Northwest by John Nicolet in 1634
With a Sketch of His Life

ISBN/EAN: 9783337014469

Printed in Europe, USA, Canada, Australia, Japan

Cover: Foto ©ninafisch / pixelio.de

More available books at **www.hansebooks.com**

HISTORY

OF THE

DISCOVERY OF THE NORTHWEST

BY

JOHN NICOLET

IN 1634

WITH A

SKETCH OF HIS LIFE

BY

C.^D W. BUTTERFIELD

Author of "Crawford's Campaign against Sandusky," "History of Wisconsin"
In Historical Atlas of the State, "The Washington-Crawford Letters,"
"History of the University of Wisconsin," etc.

CINCINNATI
ROBERT CLARKE & CO.
1881

COPYRIGHTED, 1881,
BY C. W. BUTTERFIELD.

PREFACE.

In the following pages, I have attempted to record, in a faithful manner, the indomitable perseverance and heroic bravery displayed by John Nicolet in an exploration which resulted in his being the first of civilized men to set foot upon any portion of the Northwest; that is, upon any part of the territory now constituting the States of Ohio, Indiana, Illinois, Michigan, and Wisconsin. It is shown how he brought to the knowledge of the world the existence of a "fresh-water sea"—Lake Michigan—beyond and to the westward of Lake Huron; how he visited a number of Indian nations before unheard of; how he penetrated many leagues beyond the utmost verge of previous discoveries, with an almost reckless fortitude, to bind distant tribes to French interests; and how he sought to find an ocean, which, it was believed, was not a great distance westward of the St. Lawrence, and which would prove a near route to China and Japan.

The principal sources from which I have drawn, in my investigations concerning the life and explorations of Nicolet, are the Jesuit Relations. So nearly contemporaneous are these publications with his discoveries—especially those which contain a record of them—and so trustworthy are they in their recital of facts connected therewith, that their value, in this connection, can hardly be over-estimated. Each one of the series having a particular bearing upon the subject of this narrative has been studied with a care commensurate with its importance. Other accounts of the same period, as well as of a somewhat later date, together with the researches of modern writers, concerning the daring Frenchman, whose name stands first on the list of the explorers of the Northwest, have, likewise, been carefully examined, the object being, if not to exhaust all known sources of information illustrative of these discoveries, at least to profit by them. Aid has been received, in addition, from several living authors, especially from Benjamin Sulte, Esq., of Ottawa, Canada, to whom, and to all others who have extended a helping hand, I return my sincere thanks.

C. W. B.

MADISON, WISCONSIN, 1881.

CONTENTS.

INTRODUCTION.

PAGE.

Pre-historic Man in the Northwest—The Red Race—First Discoveries in New France, ... 7

CHAPTER I.

Events Leading to Western Exploration, ... 11

CHAPTER II.

John Nicolet, the Explorer, ... 26

CHAPTER III.

Nicolet Discovers the Northwest, ... 35

CHAPTER IV.

Subsequent Career and Death of Nicolet, ... 75

Appendix, ... 93

Index, ... 107

(v)

INTRODUCTION.

PRE-HISTORIC MAN IN THE NORTHWEST—THE RED RACE—
FIRST DISCOVERIES IN NEW FRANCE.

Of the existence, in what are now the States of Ohio, Indiana, Illinois, Michigan, and Wisconsin, at a remote period, of a race superior in intelligence to the red men who inhabited this region when first seen by a European, there are indubitable evidences. Who were these ancient occupiers of the territory just mentioned—of its prairies and woodlands, hills and valleys? There are no traditions of their power, of their labor, or of their wisdom—no record of their having lived, except in rapidly-decaying relics. They left no descendants to recount their daring deeds. All that remain of them—the so-called Mound-Builders—are mouldering skeletons. All that are to be seen of their handicraft are perishing earth-works and rude implements. These sum up the "types and shadows" of the pre-historic age.

There is nothing to connect "the dark backward and abysm" of mound-building times with those of the red race of the Northwest; and all that is known of the latter dating earlier than their first discovery, is exceedingly dim and shadowy. Upon the extended area bounded by Lake Superior on the north, Lake Michigan on the east, wide-spreading prairies on the south, and the Mississippi river on the west, there met and mingled two distinct Indian families—Algonquins and Dakotas. Concerning the various tribes of these families, nothing of importance could be gleaned by the earliest explorers; at least, very little has been preserved. Tradition, it is true, pointed to the Algonquins as having, at some remote period, migrated from the east; and this has been confirmed by a study of their language. It indicated, also, that the Dakotas, at a time far beyond the memory of the most aged, came from the west or southwest—fighting their way as they came; that one of their tribes [1] once dwelt upon the shores of a sea; but when and for what purpose they left their home none could relate.

The residue of the Northwest was the dwelling-place of Algonquins alone. In reality, therefore, "the territory northwest of the river Ohio" has no veritable history ante-dating the period of its first discovery by civilized man. Portions of the country had been heard of, it is true, but only through vague reports of savages. There were no accounts at all, besides these, of the extensive region of the upper lakes or of the valley of the Upper Mississippi; while nothing whatever was known of the Ohio or of parts adjacent.

The first of the discoveries in the New World after that of Columbus, in 1492, having an immediate bearing upon this narrative, was that of John Cabot, in 1497. On the third of July, of that year, he saw what is now believed to have been the coast of Labrador. After sailing a short distance south, he probably discovered the island of Newfoundland. In 1498,

---

[1] Ancestors of the present Winnebagoes.

his son, Sebastian, explored the continent from Labrador to Virginia, and possibly as far south as Florida. Gaspar Cortereal, in 1500, reached the shore seen by John Cabot, and explored it several hundred miles. He was followed, in 1524, by John Verrazzano, who discovered the North American coast in, probably, the latitude of what is now Wilmington, North Carolina. He continued his exploration to the northward as far as Newfoundland. To the region visited by him, he gave the name of New France. The attention of the reader is now directed to some of the most important events, in the country thus named, which followed, for a period of a hundred and ten years, the voyage of Verrazzano.

HISTORY

OF THE

DISCOVERY OF THE NORTHWEST.

CHAPTER I.

EVENTS LEADING TO WESTERN EXPLORATION.

The discovery of the river St. Lawrence, and of the great lakes which pour their superabundant waters through it into the gulf, was not the least in importance of the events which signalized the opening of the history of the New World. The credit of having first spread a sail upon the majestic stream of Canada, and of obtaining such information as afterward led to a knowledge of the whole of its valley, belongs to James Cartier, a native of St. Malo—a port in the north of France. Cartier was a skillful mariner. On the twentieth of April, 1534, he sailed from his native place, under orders of the French admiral, for the coast of Newfoundland, intent on exploring unknown seas, and countries washed by them. He took with him two ships of fifty tons each, and in twenty days saw the large island lying between the ocean and the river he was soon to discover. Favorable winds had wafted him and his hundred and twenty-two sailors and adventurers to inhospitable shores, but at an auspicious season of the year.

Having sailed nearly around Newfoundland, Cartier turned to the south, and, crossing the gulf, entered a bay, which he named Des Chaleurs, because of the midsummer heats. A little farther north he landed and took possession of the country in the name of the French king. His vessels were now at anchor in the smaller inlet of Gaspé. Sailing still further north, Cartier, in August, discovered the river St. Lawrence. He moved up its channel until land was sighted on either side; then, being unprepared to remain through the winter, he sailed back again to the gulf, crossed the ocean, and moored his vessels in safety in St. Malo. He made the return voyage in less than thirty days. This was, at that period, an astonishing achievement. The success of the expedition filled the whole of France with wonder. In less than five months, the Atlantic had been crossed; a large river discovered; a new country added to the dominions of France; and the ocean recrossed. All this had been accomplished before it was generally known that an expedition had been undertaken.

The remarkable pleasantness of this summer's voyage, the narratives of Cartier and his companions, and the importance attached to their discoveries, aroused the enthusiasm of the French; and, as might be expected, a new expedition was planned. Three well-furnished ships were provided by the king. Even some of the nobility volunteered for the voyage. All were eager to cross the Atlantic. On the nineteenth of May, 1535, the squadron sailed. But Cartier had not, this time, a pleasant summer cruise. Storms raged. The ships separated. For seven weeks they buffeted the troubled ocean. Their rendezvous was the Straits of Belle Isle, which they finally reached; but the omens were bad. The adventurers had confidently looked for pleasant gales and a quick voyage, and these expectations had all been blasted. Now, however, they arrived within sight of Newfoundland, and their spirits rose. Carried to the west of that island, on the day of Saint Lawrence, they gave the name of that martyr to a portion of the gulf which opened before them. The name was afterward given to the whole of that body of water and to the river Cartier had previously discovered. Sailing to the north of Anticosti, they ascended the St. Lawrence, reaching, in September, a fine harbor in an island since called Orleans.

Leaving his two largest ships in the waters of the river now known as the St. Charles, Cartier, with the smallest and two open boats, ascended the St. Lawrence until a considerable Indian village was reached, situated on an island called Hochelaga. Standing upon the summit of a hill, on this island, and looking away up the river, the commander had fond imaginings of future glory awaiting his countrymen in colonizing this region. "He called the hill Mont-Réal, and time, that has transferred the name of the island, is realizing his visions;" for on that island now stands the city of Montreal. While at Hochelaga, Cartier gathered some indistinct accounts of the surrounding country, and of the river Ottawa coming down from the hills of the Northwest. Rejoining his ships, he spent the winter in a palisaded fort on the bank of the St. Charles, with his vessels moored before it.

The cold was intense. Many of his men died of scurvy. Early in the spring, possession was again taken of the country in the name of the French king; and, on the sixteenth of July, 1536, the Breton mariner dropped anchor in St. Malo—he having returned in two ships; the other was abandoned, and three hundred and twelve years after was discovered imbedded in mud. France was disappointed. Hopes had been raised too high. Expectations had not been realized. Further explorations, therefore, were, for the time, postponed.

Notwithstanding the failure of Cartier's second voyage, the great valley of the St. Lawrence was not to remain very long unknown to the world, in any of its parts. It was thought unworthy a gallant nation to abandon the enterprise; and one more trial at exploration and colonization was determined upon. Again the bold mariner of St. Malo started for the St. Lawrence. This was on the twenty-third of May, 1541. He took with him five ships; but he went, unfortunately, as subordinate, in some respects, to John Francis de la Roque, Lord of Roberval, a nobleman of Picardy, whom the king of France had appointed viceroy of the country now again to be visited. The object of the enterprise was declared to be discovery, settlement, and the conversion of the Indians. Cartier was the first to sail. Again he entered the St. Lawrence.

After erecting a fort near the site of the present city of Quebec, Cartier ascended the river in two boats to explore the rapids above the island of Hochelaga. He then returned and passed the winter at his fort; and, in the spring, not having heard from the viceroy,

EVENTS LEADING TO WESTERN EXPLORATION. 15

he set sail for France. In June, 1542, in the harbor of St. John, he met the Lord of Roberval, outward bound, with three ships and two hundred men. The viceroy ordered Cartier to return to the St. Lawrence; but the mariner of St. Malo escaped in the night, and continued his voyage homeward. Roberval, although abandoned by his subordinate, once more set sail. After wintering in the St. Lawrence, he, too, abandoned the country—giving back his immense viceroyalty to the rightful owners.

In 1578, there were three hundred and fifty fishing vessels at Newfoundland belonging to the French, Spanish, Portuguese, and English; besides these were a number—twenty or more—of Biscayan whalers. The Marquis de la Roche, a Catholic nobleman of Brittany, encouraged by Henry IV., undertook the colonization of New France, in 1598. But the ill-starred attempt resulted only in his leaving forty convicts to their fate on Sable island, off the coast of Nova Scotia. Of their number, twelve only were found alive five years subsequent to La Roche's voyage. In 1599, another expedition was resolved on. This was undertaken by Pontgravé, a merchant of St. Malo, and Chauvin, a captain of the marine. In consideration of a monopoly of the fur-trade, granted them by the king of France, these men undertook to establish a colony of five hundred persons in New France. At Tadoussac, at the mouth of the Saguenay, they built a cluster of wooden huts and store-houses, where sixteen men were left to gather furs; these either died or were scattered among the Indians before the return of the spring of 1601. Chauvin made a second voyage to Tadoussac, but failed to establish a permanent settlement. During a third voyage he died, and his enterprise perished with him.

In 1603, a company of merchants of France was formed, and Samuel Champlain, with a small band of adventurers, dispatched, in two small vessels, to make a preliminary survey of the St. Lawrence. He reached the valley in safety, sailed past the lofty promontory on which Quebec now stands, and proceeded onward to the island of Hochelaga, where his vessels where anchored. In a skiff, with a few Indians, Champlain vainly endeavored to pass the rapids of the great river. The baffled explorer returned to his ships. From the savages, he gleaned some information of ulterior regions. The natives drew for him rude plans of the river above, and its lakes and cataracts. His curiosity was inflamed, and he resolved one day to visit the country so full of natural wonders. Now, however, he was constrained to return to France. He had accomplished the objects of his mission—the making of a brief exploration of the valley of the chief river of Canada.

It was the opinion of Champlain that on the banks of the St. Lawrence was the true site of a settlement; that here a fortified post should be erected; that thence, by following up the waters of the interior region to their sources, a western route might be traced to China, the distance being estimated by him at not more than two or three hundred leagues; and that the fur-trade of the whole country might be secured to France by the erection of a fort at some point commanding the river. These views, five years subsequent to his visit to the St. Lawrence, induced the fitting out of a second expedition, for trade, exploration, and colonization. On the thirteenth of April, 1608, Champlain again sailed—this time with men, arms, and stores for a colony. The fur-trade was intrusted to another. The mouth of the Saguenay was reached in June; and, soon after, a settlement was commenced on the brink of the St. Lawrence—the site of the present market-place of the lower town of Quebec. A rigorous winter and great suffering followed. Supplies arrived in the spring, and Champlain determined to enter upon his long-meditated explorations;—the only obstacles in the way were the savage nations he would every-where meet. He would be compelled to resort to diplomacy—to unite a friendly tribe to his interests, and, thus strengthened, to conquer, by force of arms, the hostile one.

The tribes of the Hurons, who dwelt on the lake which now bears their name, and their allies, the Algonquins, upon the Ottawa and the St. Lawrence, Champlain learned, were at war with the Iroquois, or Five Nations, whose homes were within the present State of New York. In June, 1609, he advanced, with sixty Hurons and Algonquins and two white men, up what is now known as the Richelieu river to the discovery of the first of the great lakes—the one which now bears his name. Upon its placid waters, this courageous band was stopped by a war-party of Iroquois. On shore, the contending forces met, when a few discharges of an arquebuse sent the advancing enemy in wild dismay back into the forest. The victory was complete. Promptly Champlain returned to the St. Lawrence, and his allies to their homes, not, however, until the latter had invited the former

2

to visit their towns and aid them again in their wars. Champlain then revisited France, but the year 1610 found him once more in the St. Lawrence, with two objects in view: one, to proceed northward, to explore Hudson's bay; the other, to go westward, and examine the great lakes and the mines of copper on their shores, of the existence of which he had just been informed by the savages; for he was determined he would never cease his explorations until he had penetrated to the western sea, or that of the north, so as to open the way to China. But, after fighting a battle with the Iroquois at the mouth of the river Richelieu, he gave up, for the time, all thought of further exploration, and returned to France.

On the thirteenth of May, 1611, Champlain again arrived in the St. Lawrence. To secure the advantages of the fur-trade to his superiors was now his principal object; and, to that end, he chose the site of the present city of Montreal for a post, which he called Place Royale. Soon afterward, he returned to France; but, early in the spring of 1613, the tireless voyager again crossed the Atlantic, and sailed up the St. Lawrence; this time bound for the Ottawa to discover the North sea. After making his way up that river to the home of the Algonquins of Isle des Allumettes, he returned in disgust to the St. Lawrence, and again embarked for France.

At the site of the present city of Montreal, there had assembled, in the summer of 1615, Hurons from their distant villages upon the shores of their great lake, and Algonquins from their homes on the Ottawa—come down to a yearly trade with the French upon the St. Lawrence. Champlain, who had re-

EVENTS LEADING TO WESTERN EXPLORATION. 19

turned in May from France, was asked by the assembled savages to join their bands against the Iroquois. He consented; but, while absent at Quebec, making needful preparations, the savages became impatient, and departed for their homes. With them went Father Joseph le Caron, a Récollet, accompanied by twelve armed Frenchmen. It was the intention of this missionary to learn the language of the Hurons, and labor for their spiritual welfare. His departure from the St. Lawrence was on the first day of July. Nine days afterward, Champlain, with two Frenchmen and ten Indians followed him. Both parties traveled up the Ottawa to the Algonquin villages; passed the two lakes of the Allumettes; threaded their way to a well-trodden portage, crossing which brought them to Lake Nipissing; thence, they floated westward down the current of French river, to what is now known as Georgian bay; afterward, for more than a hundred miles, they journeyed southward along the eastern shores of that bay to its head; and there was the home of the Hurons.

Champlain, with a naked host of allies, was soon on the march against the Iroquois from the Huron villages, moving down the river Trent, as since named, to its mouth, when his eyes were gladdened with the view of another of the fresh water seas—Lake Ontario. Boldly they crossed its broad expanse, meeting the enemy at a considerable distance inland from its southern shores. Defensive works of the Iroquois defied the assaults of the beseigers. The Huron warriors returned in disgust to their homes, taking Champlain with them. He was compelled to spend the winter as the guest of these savages, returning to the St. Lawrence by way of the Ottawa, and reaching Quebec on the eleventh of July, 1616. He had seen enough of the region traversed by him to know that there was an immense country lying to the westward ready to be given to his king the moment he should be able to explore and make it known. Father le Caron, who had preceded Champlain on his outward trip to the Huron villages, also preceded him on his return; but he remained long enough with those Indians to obtain a considerable knowledge of their language and of their manners and customs.

Quebec, at this period, could hardly be called a settlement. It contained a population of fur-traders and friars of fifty or sixty persons. It had a fort, and Champlain was the nominal commander. In the interest of the infant colony he went every year to France. His was the duty to regulate the monopoly of the company of merchants in their trade with the Indians. In the summer of 1622, the Iroquois beset the settlement, but made no actual attack. A change was now at hand in the affairs of New France. Two Huguenots, William and Émery de Caen, had taken the place of the old company of St. Malo and Rouen, but were afterward compelled to share their monopoly with them. Fresh troubles were thus introduced into the infant colony, not only in religious affairs, but in secular matters. The Récollets had previously established five missions, extending from Acadia to the borders of Lake Huron. Now, three Jesuits— among their number John de Brébeuf—arrived in the colony, and began their spiritual labors. This was in 1625. When the year 1627 was reached, the settlement at Quebec had a population of about one hundred persons—men, women, and children. The chief trading stations upon the St. Lawrence were Quebec, Three Rivers, the Rapids of St. Louis, and Tadoussac. Turning our eyes to the western wilds, we see that the Hurons, after the return of Le Caron, were not again visited by missionaries until 1622.

In the year 1627, the destinies of France were held by Cardinal Richelieu as in the hollow of his hand. He had constituted himself grand master and superintendent of navigation and commerce. By him the privileges of the Caens were annulled, and a company formed, consisting of a hundred associates, called the Company of New France. At its head was Richelieu himself. Louis the Thirteenth made over to this company forever the fort and settlement at Quebec, and all the territory of New France, including Florida. To them was given power to appoint judges, build fortresses, cast cannon, confer titles, and concede lands. They were to govern in peace and in war. Their monopoly of the fur-trade was made perpetual; while that of all other commerce within the limits of their government was limited to fifteen years, except that the whale-fishery and the cod-fishery were to remain open to all. They could take whatever steps they might think expedient or proper for the protection of the colony and the fostering of trade. It will thus be seen that the Hundred Associates had conferred upon them almost sovereign power. For fifteen years their commerce was not to be troubled with duties or imposts. Partners, whether nobles, officers, or ecclesiastics, might engage in commercial pursuits without derogating from the privileges of their order. To all these benefits the king added a donation of two ships of war. Of this powerful association, Champlain was one of the members.

In return for these privileges conferred, behold how little these hundred partners were compelled to perform. They engaged to convoy to New France, during 1628, two or three hundred men of all trades, and before the year 1643 to increase the number to four thousand persons of both sexes; to supply all their settlers with lodging, food, clothing, and farm implements, for three years; then they would allow them sufficient land to support themselves, cleared to a certain extent; and would also furnish them the grain necessary for sowing it; stipulating, also, that the emigrants should be native Frenchmen and Roman Catholics, and none others; and, finally, agreeing to settle three priests in each settlement, whom they were bound to provide with every article necessary for their personal comfort, and to defray the expenses of their ministerial labors for fifteen years. After the expiration of that time, cleared lands were to be granted by the company to the clergy for maintaining the Roman Catholic Church in New France. It was thus that the Hundred Associates became proprietors of the whole country claimed by France, from Florida to the Arctic Circle; from Newfoundland to the sources of the St. Lawrence and its tributaries. Meanwhile, the fur-trade had brought a considerable knowledge of the Ottawa, and of the country of the Hurons, to the French upon the St. Lawrence, through the yearly visits of the savages from those distant parts and the journeyings of the fur-trader in quest of peltry.

In April, 1628, the first vessels of the Hundred Associates sailed from France with colonists and supplies bound for the St. Lawrence. Four of these vessels were armed. Every thing seemed propitious for a speedy arrival at Quebec, where the inhabitants were sorely pressed for food; but a storm, which had for some time been brewing in Europe, broke in fury upon New France. The imprudent zeal of the Catholics in England, and the persecution of the Huguenots in France, aroused the English, who determined to conquer the French possessions in North America, if possible; and, to that end, they sent out David Kirk, with an armed squadron, to attack the settlements in Canada. The fleet reached the harbor of Tadoussac before the arrival of the vessels of the Company of New France. Kirk sent a demand for the surrender of Quebec, but Champlain determined to defend the place; at least, he resolved to make a show of defense; and the English commander thought best not to attack such a formidable looking position. All the supplies sent by the Hundred Associates to the St. Lawrence were captured or sunk; and the next year, after most of its inhabitants had dispersed in the forests for food, Quebec surrendered. England thus gained her first supremacy upon the great river of Canada.

The terms of the capitulation were that the French were to be conveyed to their own country; and each soldier was allowed to take with him furs to the value of twenty crowns. As some had lately returned from the Hurons with peltry of no small value, their loss was considerable. The French prisoners, including Champlain, were conveyed across the ocean by Kirk, but their arrival in England was after a treaty of peace had been signed between the two powers. The result was, the restoration of New France to the French crown; and, on the 5th of July, 1632, Émery de Caen cast anchor at Quebec to reclaim the country. He had received a commission to hold, for one year, a monopoly of the fur-trade, as an indemnity for his losses in the war; after which time he was to give place to the Hundred Associates. The missions in Canada which by the success of the British arms had been interrupted, were now to be continued by Jesuits alone. De Caen brought with him two of that order—Paul le Jeune and Anne de la Noue.

On the twenty-third of May, 1633, Champlain, commissioned anew by Richelieu, resumed command at Quebec, in behalf of the Hundred Partners, arriving out with considerable supplies and several new settlers. With him returned the Jesuit father, John de Brébeuf. The Récollets had been virtually ejected from Canada. The whole missionary field was now ready for cultivation by the followers of Loyola. New France was restored to Champlain and his company, and to Catholicism.

Champlain's first care was to place the affairs of the colony in a more prosperous condition, and establish a better understanding with the Indians. In both respects, he was tolerably successful. His knowledge of the western country had been derived from his own observations during the tours of 1613 and 1615, but especially from accounts given him by the Indians. At the beginning of 1634, the whole French population, from Gaspé to Three Rivers, was hardly one hundred and fifty souls, mostly engaged in the trading business, on behalf of the Hundred Partners, whose operations were carried on principally at the point last named and at Tadoussac—sometimes as far up the St. Lawrence as the site of the present city of Montreal, but not often. Of the small colony upon the great river of Canada, Champlain was the heart and soul. The interior of the continent was yet to be explored. He was resolved to know more of ulterior regions—to create more friends among the savages therein. The time had arrived for such enterprises, and a trusty conductor was at hand.

CHAPTER II.

JOHN NICOLET, THE EXPLORER.

As early as the year 1615, Champlain had selected a number of young men and put them in care of some of his Indian friends, to have them trained to the life of the woods—to the language, manners, customs, and habits of the savages. His object was to open, through them, as advisers and interpreters, friendly relations, when the proper time should come, with the Indian nations not yet brought in close alliance with the French. In 1618, an opportunity presented itself for him to add another young Frenchman to the list of those who had been sent to be trained in all the mysteries of savage life; for, in that year, John Nicolet[1] arrived from France, and was dispatched to the woods.[2] The new-comer was born in Cherbourg,

---

[1] The proper spelling is "Nicolet," not "Nicollet," nor "Nicollett." The correct pronunciation is "Nick-o-lay." The people of the province of Quebec all pronounce the name "Nicoll*ette*," though improperly, the same as the word would be pronounced by English-speaking people if it were spelled "Nick-o-let." But it is now invariably written by them "Nicolet."

[2] Vimont, *Relation*, 1643 (Quebec edition, 1858), p. 3. The Jesuits, intent upon pushing their fields of labor far into the heart of the continent, let slip no opportunity after their arrival upon the St. Lawrence to inform themselves concerning ulterior regions; and the information thus obtained was noted down by them.

JOHN NICOLET, THE EXPLORER. 27

in Normandy. His father, Thomas Nicolet, was a mail-carrier from that city to Paris. His mother's name was Marguerite de la Mer.[1]

Nicolet was a young man of good character, endowed with a profound religious feeling, and an ex-

---

They minutely described, during a period of forty years, beginning with the year 1632, the various tribes they came in contact with; and their hopes and fears as to Christianizing them were freely expressed. Accounts of their journeys were elaborated upon, and their missionary work put upon record. Prominent persons, as well as important events, shared their attention. Details concerning the geography of the country were also written out. The intelligence thus collected was sent every summer by the superiors to the provincials at Paris, where it was yearly published, in the French language. Taken together, these publications constitute what are known as the *Jesuit Relations*. They have been collected and republished in the same language, at Quebec, by the Canadian government, in three large volumes. As these are more accessible to the general reader in this form than in the original (Cramoisy) editions, they are cited in this narrative.

There is no complete translation of the *Relations* into the English language. Numerous extracts from the originals bearing particularly upon the West—especially upon what is now Wisconsin—were made some years since by Cyrus Woodman, of Mineral Point, translations of which are to be found in Smith's history of that State, Vol. III., pp. 10-112. But none of these are from the *Relation* of 1643—the most important one in its reference to Nicolet and his visit to the Northwest.

[1] "Jean Nicollet né à Cherbourg, était fils de Thomas Nicollet, messager ordinaire de Cherbourg à Paris, et de Marie La Mer." —Ferland's *Cours d' Histoire du Canada* (1861), Vol. I., p. 324, note. But, in his "Notes sur les Registres de Notre-Dame de Québec" (Quebec, 1863, p. 30), he corrects the mother's name, giving it as in the text above. That this was her real name is ascertained from the Quebec parochial register, and from Guitet's records (notary) of that city.

cellent memory. He awakened in the breast of
Champlain high hopes of usefulness, and was by him
sent to the Algonquins of Isle des Allumettes, in the Ottawa river. These Indians were the same Algonquins
that were visited by Champlain in 1613. They are
frequently spoken of, in early annals of Canada, as
Algonquins of the Isle. But all Algonquins, wherever found, were afterward designated as Ottawas by
the French. To "the Nation of the Isle," then, was
sent the young Norman, that he might learn their
language, which was in general use upon the Ottawa
river and upon the north bank of the St. Lawrence.
With them he remained two years, following them in
their wanderings, partaking of their dangers, their
fatigues, and their privations, with a courage and
fortitude equal to the boldest and the bravest of the
tribe. During all this time, he saw not the face of a
single white man. On several different occasions he
passed a number of days without a morsel of food,
and he was sometimes fain to satisfy the cravings of
hunger by eating bark.[1]

---

[1] "Il [Nicolet] arriua en la Nouuelle France, l'an mil six cents
dixhuict. Son humeur et sa memoire excellente firent esperer
quelque chose de bon de luy; ou l'enuoya hiuerner auec les Algonquins de l'Isle afin d'apprendre leur langue. Il y demeura
deux ans seul de François, accompagnant tousiours les Barbares
dans leurs courses et voyages, auec des fatigues qui ne sont imaginables qu'à ceux qui les ont veües; il passa plusieurs fois les
sept et huict iours sans rien manger, il fut sept semaines entieres
sans autre nourriture qu'vn peu d'escorce de bois."—Vimont Relation, 1643, p. 3. (The antiquated orthography and accentuation
of the Relations are strictly followed in the foregoing extract;

Nicolet, while residing with the Algonquins of Isle des Allumettes, with whose language he had now become familiar, accompanied four hundred of those savages upon a mission of peace to the Iroquois. The voyage proved a successful one, Nicolet returning in safety. Afterward, he took up his residence among the Nipissings, with whom he remained eight or nine years. He was recognized as one of the nation. He entered into the very frequent councils of those savages. He had his own cabin and establishment, doing his own fishing and trading. He had become, indeed, a naturalized **Nipissing**.[1] The mental activity

---

so, also, in all those hereafter made from them in this narrative.)

"On his [Nicolet's] first arrival [in New France], by orders of those who presided over the French colony of Quebec, he spent two whole years among the Algonquins of the island, for the purpose of learning their language, without any Frenchman as companion, and in the midst of those hardships, which may be readily conceived, if we will reflect what it must be to pass severe winters in the woods, under a covering of cedar or birch bark; to have one's means of subsistence dependent upon hunting; to be perpetually hearing rude outcries; to be deprived of the pleasant society of one's own people; and to be constantly exposed, not only to derision and insulting words, but even to daily peril of life. There was a time, indeed, when he went without food for a whole week; and (what is really wonderful) he even spent seven weeks without having any thing to eat but a little bark."—Du Creux, *Historia Canadensis*, Paris, 1664, p. 359. "Probably," says Margry, "he must, from time to time, have added some of the lichen which the Canadians call rock tripe."—*Journal Général de l'Instruction Publique*, Paris, 1862.

[1] "Il [Nicolet] accompagna quatre cents Algonquins, qui alloient en ce temps là faire la paix auec les Hiroquois, et en vint à bout

displayed by him while sojourning among these savages may be judged of from the circumstance of his having taken notes descriptive of the habits, manners, customs, and numbers of the Nipissing Indians, written in the form of memoirs, which were afterward presented by him to one of the missionaries, who, doubtless, made good use of them in after-time in giving an account of the nation.[1]

Nicolet finally left the savages, and returned to civilization, being recalled by the government and employed as commissary and Indian interpreter.[2] It is probable, however, that he had signified his desire to leave the Nipissings, as he could not live without the sacraments,[3] which were denied him so long as he remained with them, there being no mission established in their country.[4]

---

heureusement. Pleust à Dieu qu'elle n'eust iamais esté rompuë, nous ne souffririons pas à present les calamitez qui nous font gemir et donneront vn estrange empeschement à la conuersion de ces peuples. Apes cette paix faite, il alla demeurer huict ou neuf ans auec la nation des Nipisiriniens, Algonquins; là il passoit pour vn de cette nation, entrant dans les conseils forts frequents à ces peuples, ayant sa cabane et son mesnage à part, faisant sa perche et sa traitte."—Vimont, *Relation*, 1643, p. 3.

[1] "I'ay quelques memoires de sa main, qui pourront paroistre vn iour, touchant les Nipisiriniens, auec lesquels il a souuent hyuerné."—Le Jeune, *Relation*, 1636, p. 58.

[2] "Il [*Nicolet*] fut enfin rappallé et estably Commis et Interprete."—Vimont, *Relation*, 1643, p. 3.

[3] "Il [*Nicolet*] . . . ne s'en est retiré, que pour mettre son salut en asseurance dans l'vsage des Sacremens, faute desquels il y a grande risque pour l'âme, parmy les Sauuages."—Le Jeune, *Relation*, 1636, pp. 57, 58.

[4] It would be quite impossible to reconcile the *Relation* of 1643

Quebec having been reoccupied by the French, Nicolet took up his residence there. He was in high favor with Champlain, who could not but admire his remarkable adaptation to savage life—the result of his courage and peculiar temperament; at least, this admiration may be presumed, from the circumstance of his having, as the sequel shows, soon after sent him upon an important mission.

Whether Nicolet visited Quebec during his long residence among the Nipissing Indians is not known. Possibly he returned to the St. Lawrence in 1628, to receive orders from Champlain on account of the new state of things inaugurated by the creation of the system of 1627—the Hundred Associates; but, in that event, he must have soon returned, for it is known that he remained with the Nipissings during the occupation of Quebec by the English—from July, 1629, to July, 1632. The month during which, in the early days of New France, the trade of the Ottawa was performed on the St. Lawrence, was July; and, in 1632, this trade was largely carried on where the city of Three Rivers now stands, but which was not then founded.[1] The flotilla of bark canoes used to

---

(p. 3) with that of 1636 (pp. 57, 58), respecting Nicolet's retiring from his Indian life, unless he, for the motive stated, asked for his recall and was recalled accordingly.

[1] Champlain's map of 1632 shows no habitation on the St. Lawrence above Quebec. In 1633, Three Rivers was virtually founded; but the fort erected there by Champlain was not begun until 1634.—Sulte's *Chronique Trifluvienne*, p. 5.

"As for the towns in Canada, there are but three of any considerable figure. These are Quebec, Montreal, and Trois Rivieres [Three Rivers]. . . . Trois Rivieres is a town so named from

spend usually from eight to ten days in that place—seldom reaching Quebec. In the month and the year just mentioned, De Caen arrived in Canada; and he was, therefore, in the position to send word, by the assembled Indians, to the French who were living among the savages upon the Ottawa and the Georgian bay of Lake Huron, requesting their return to the St. Lawrence.

Champlain, in June, 1633, caused a small fort to be erected about forty miles above Quebec, for the rendezvous of the trading flotilla descending the St. Lawrence—to draw the market nearer Quebec. It was thus the St. Croix fort was established where the trade with the Indians would be much less likely to

---

its situation at the confluence of three rivers, one whereof is that of St. Lawrence, and lies almost in the midway between Quebec and Montreal. It is said to be a well-built town, and considerable mart, where the Indians exchange their skins and furs for European goods."—*An Account of the French Settlements in North America, Boston,* 1746, pp. 12, 14.

"Three Rivers, or Trois Rivieres, is a town of Canada East, at the confluence of the rivers St. Maurice and St. Lawrence, ninety miles from Quebec, with which it is connected by electric telegraph, and on the line of the proposed railway thence to Montreal. It is one of the oldest towns in Canada, and was long stationary as regarded enterprise or improvement; but recently it has become one of the most prosperous places in the province —a change produced principally by the commencement of an extensive trade in lumber on the river St. Maurice and its tributaries, which had heretofore been neglected, and also by increased energy in the manufacture of iron-ware, for which the St. Maurice forges, about three miles distant from the town, have always been celebrated in Canada. Three Rivers is the residence of a Roman Catholic bishop, whose diocese bears the same name; and contains a Roman Catholic cathedral, a church

be interrupted by incursions of the Iroquois than at
Three Rivers. At this time, one hundred and fifty
Huron canoes arrived at the newly-chosen position,
for traffic with the French. Possibly so great a number was the result of the change in the government
of the colony—the return of the French to Quebec the
preceding year. With this large fleet of canoes
Nicolet probably returned to civilization; for it is
certain that he was upon the St. Lawrence as early as
June, 1634, ready to embark in an undertaking which,
of necessity, would have caused so much consultation
and preparation as to preclude the idea of his arrival,
just then, from the Ottawa. An Indian interpreter
—one well acquainted with the Algonquins of the
Ottawa, and to a certain extent with the Hurons of
Georgian bay—who could Champlain more safely depend upon than Nicolet to develop his schemes of
exploration in the unknown western country, the
door of which he had himself opened in previous
years? Who was there better qualified than his
young *protégé*, familiar as he was with the Algonquin
and Huron-Iroquois tongues, to hold "talks" with
savage tribes still further west, and smoke with them
the pipe of peace—to the end that a nearer route to

---

of England, a Scotch kirk, and a Wesleyan chapel, an Ursuline
convent, with a school attached, where over two hundred young
females are educated; two public and several private schools,
a mechanics' institute, a Canadian institute, and a Young Men's
Improvement, and several other societies. It sends a member
to the provincial parliament. Population in 1852, was 4,966; in
1861, 6,058. The district of Three Rivers embraces both sides
of the St. Lawrence, and is subdivided into four counties."—
Lippincott's Gazetteer, Philadelphia, 1874.

China and Japan might be discovered; or, at least, that the fur-trade might be made more profitable to the Hundred Associates? Surely, no one. Hence it was that Nicolet was recalled by the governor of Canada.

CHAPTER III.

NICOLET DISCOVERS THE NORTHWEST.

Notwithstanding Champlain had previously ascended the Ottawa and stood upon the shores of the Georgian bay of Lake Huron, and although he had received from western Indians numerous reports of distant regions, his knowledge of the great lakes was, in 1634, exceedingly limited. He had heard of Niagara, but was of the opinion that it was only a rapid, such as the St. Louis, in the river St. Lawrence. He was wholly uninformed concerning Lake Erie, Lake St. Clair, and Lake Michigan; while, of Lake Huron, he knew little, and of Lake Superior still less. He was assured that there was a connection between the last-named lake and the St. Lawrence; but his supposition was, that a river flowed from Lake Huron directly into Lake Ontario. Such, certainly was the extent of his information in 1632, as proven by his map of that date;[1] and that, for the

---

[1] This map was the first attempt at delineating the great lakes. The original was, beyond a reasonable doubt, the work of Champlain himself. So much of New France as had been visited by the delineator is given with some degree of accuracy. On the whole, the map has a grotesque appearance, yet it possesses much value. It shows where many savage nations were located at its date. By it, several important historical problems concerning the Northwest are solved. It

next two years, he could have received much additional information concerning the great lakes is not probable.

He had early been told that near the borders of one of these "fresh-water seas," were copper mines; for, in June, 1610, while moving up the St. Lawrence to join a war-party of Algonquins, Hurons, and Montagnais, he met, after ascending the river about twenty-five miles above Quebec, a canoe containing two Indians—an Algonquin and a Montagnais—who had been dispatched to urge him to hasten forward with all possible speed. He entertained them on his bark, and conferred with them about many matters concerning their wars. Thereupon, the Algonquin savage drew from a sack a piece of copper, a foot long, which he gave Champlain. It was very handsome and quite pure. He said there were large quantities of the metal where he obtained the piece, and that it was found on the bank of a river near a great lake. He also declared that the Indians gathered it in lumps, and, having melted it, spread it in sheets, smoothing it with stones.[1]

Champlain had, also, early information that there

---

was first published, along with Champlain's "Voyages de la Novvelle France," in Paris. Fac-similes have been published; one accompanies volume third of E. B. O'Callaghan's "Documentary History of the State of New York," Albany, 1850; another is found in a reprint of Champlain's works by Laverdiere (Vol. VI.), Quebec, 1870; another is by Tross, Paris.

[1] Champlain's *Voyages*, Paris, 1613. pp. 246, 247. Upon his map of 1632, Champlain marks an island "where there is a copper mine." Instead of being placed in Lake Superior, as it doubtless should have been, it finds a location in Green bay.

dwelt in those far-off countries a nation which once lived upon the borders of a distant sea. These people were called, for that reason, "Men of the Sea," by the Algonquins. Their homes were less than four hundred leagues away. It was likewise reported that another people, without hair or beards, whose costumes and manners somewhat resembled the Tartars, came from the west to trade with this "sea-tribe." These more remote traders, as was claimed, made their journeys upon a great water in large canoes. The missionaries among the Hurons, as well as Champlain and the best informed of the French settlers upon the St. Lawrence, thought this "great water" must be a western sea leading to Asia.[1] Some of the Indians who traded with the French were in the habit of going occasionally to barter with those "People of the Sea," distant from their homes five or six weeks' journey. A lively imagination on part of the French easily converted these hairless traders coming from the west into Chinese or Japanese; although, in fact, they were none other than the progenitors of the savages now known as the Sioux,[2]

---

[1] This "great water" was, as will hereafter be shown, the Mississippi and its tributary, the Wisconsin.

[2] Synonyms: Cioux, Scious, Sioust, Naduessue, Nadouesiouack, Nadouesiouck, Nadoussi, Nadouessioux, etc.

"The Sioux, or Dakotah [Dakota], . . . were [when first visited by civilized men] a numerous people, separated into three great divisions, which were again subdivided into bands. . . . [One of these divisions—the most easterly—was the Issanti.] The other great divisions, the Yanktons and the Tintonwans, or Tetons, lived west of the Mississippi, extending beyond the Missouri, and ranging as far as the Rocky Mountains. The Issanti cultivated

while the "sea-tribe" was the nation called, subsequently, Winnebagoes.[1] Upon these reports, the

the soil; but the extreme western bands lived upon the buffalo alone. . . .

"The name Sioux is an abbreviation of *Nadouessioux*, an Ojibwa [Chippewa] word, meaning *enemies*. The Ojibwas used it to designate this people, and occasionally, also, the Iroquois—being at deadly war with both."—Parkman's "La Salle and the Discovery of the Great West" (revised ed.), p. 242, note.

[1] From the Algonquin word "ouinipeg," signifying "bad smelling water," as salt-water was by them designated. When, therefore, the Algonquins spoke of this tribe as the "Ouinipigou," they simply meant "Men of the Salt-water;" that is, "Men of the Sea." But the French gave a different signification to the word, calling the nation "Men of the Stinking-water;" or, rather, "the Nation of Stinkards"—"la Nation des Puans." And they are so designated by Champlain in his "Voyages," in 1632, and on his map of that year. By Friar Gabriel Sagard ("Histoire du Canada," Paris, 1636 p. 201), they are also noted as "des Puants." Sagard's information of the Winnebagoes, although printed after Nicolet's visit to that tribe, was obtained previous to that event. The home of this nation was around the head of Green bay, in what is now the State of Wisconsin. Says Vimont (*Relation*, 1640, p. 35), as to the signification of the word "ouinipeg:"

"Quelques François les appellant la Nation des Puans, à cause que le mot Algonquin ouinipeg signifie eau puante; or ils nomment ainsi l'eau de la mer salée, si bien que ces peuples se nomment Ouinipigou, pource qu'ils viennent des bords d'vne mer dont nous n'auons point de cognoissance, et par consequent il ne faut pas les appeller la nation des Puans, mais la nation de la mer." The same is reiterated in the *Relations* of 1648 and 1654. Consult, in this connection, Smith's "History of Wisconsin," Vol. III., pp. 11, 15, 17. To John Gilmary Shea belongs the credit of first identifying the "Ouinipigou," or "Gens de Mer," of Vimont (*Relation*, 1640), with the Winnebagoes. See his "Discovery and Exploration of the Mississippi Valley, 1853, pp. 20, 21.

missionaries had already built fond expectations of one day reaching China by the ocean which washed alike the shores of Asia and America. And, as already noticed, Champlain, too, was not less sanguine in his hopes of accomplishing a similar journey.

Nicolet, while living with the Nipissings, must have heard many stories of the strange people so much resembling the Chinese, and doubtless his curiosity was not less excited than was Champlain's. But the great question was, who should penetrate the wilderness to the "People of the Sea"—to "La Nation des Puants," as they were called by Champlain? Naturally enough, the eyes of the governor of Canada were fixed upon Nicolet as the man to make the trial. The latter had returned to Quebec, it will be remembered, and was acting as commissary and interpreter for the Hundred Associates. That he was paid by them and received his orders from them through Champlain, their representative, is reasonably certain. So he was chosen to make a journey to the Winnebagoes, for the purpose, principally, of solving the problem of a near route to China.[1]

If he should fail in discovering a new highway to the east in reaching these "People of the Sea," it would, in any event, be an important step toward the exploration of the then unknown west; and why should not the explorer, in visiting the various nations living upon the eastern and northern shores of

---

[1] It is nowhere stated in the *Relations* that such was the object of Champlain in dispatching Nicolet to these people; nevertheless, that it was the chief purpose had in view by him, is fairly deducible from what is known of his purposes at that date. He had, also, other designs to be accomplished.

Lake Huron, and beyond this inland sea, create friends among the savage tribes, in hopes that a regular trade in peltries might be established with them. To this end, he must meet them in a friendly way; have talks with them; and firmly unite them, if possible, to French interests. Champlain knew, from personal observation made while traveling upon the Ottawa and the shores of the Georgian bay of Lake Huron—from the reports of savages who came from their homes still further westward, and from what fur-traders, missionaries, and the young men sent by him among the savages to learn their languages (of whom Nicolet himself was a notable example) had heard that there were comparatively easy facilities of communication by water between the upper country and the St. Lawrence. He knew, also, that the proper time had come to send a trusty ambassador to these far-off nations; so, by the end of June, 1634, Nicolet, at Quebec, was ready to begin his eventful journey, at the command of Champlain.

"Opposite Quebec lies the tongue of land called Point Levi. One who, in the summer of the year 1634, stood on its margin and looked northward, across the St. Lawrence, would have seen, at the distance of a mile or more, a range of lofty cliffs, rising on the left into the bold heights of Cape Diamond, and on the right sinking abruptly to the bed of the tributary river St. Charles. Beneath these cliffs, at the brink of the St. Lawrence, he would have descried a cluster of warehouses, sheds, and wooden tenements. Immediately above, along the verge of the precipice, he could have traced the outlines of a fortified work, with a flag-staff and a few small cannon to command the river; while, at the only point where nature had made the heights accessible, a zigzag path connected the warehouses and the fort.

"Now, embarked in the canoe of some Montagnais Indian, let him cross the St. Lawrence, land at the pier, and, passing the cluster of buildings, climb the pathway up the cliff. Pausing for a rest and breath, he might see, ascending and descending, the tenants of this out-post of the wilderness: a soldier of the fort, or an officer in slouched hat and plume; a factor of the fur company, owner and sovereign lord of all Canada; a party of Indians; a trader from the upper country, one of the precursors of that hardy race of *coureurs de bois*, destined to form a conspicuous and striking feature of the Canadian population: next, perhaps, would appear a figure widely different. The close, black cassock, the rosary hanging from the waist, and the wide, black hat, looped up at the sides, proclaimed the Jesuit."[1]

There were in Canada, at this date, six of these Jesuits—Le Jeune, Masse, De Noüe, Daniel, Davost, and Brébeuf; to the last three had been assigned the Huron mission. On the first day of July, 1634, Daniel and Brébeuf left Quebec for Three Rivers, where they were to meet some Hurons. Davost followed three days after. About the same time another expedition started up the St. Lawrence, destined for the same place, to erect a fort. The Jesuits were bound for the scene of their future labors in the Huron country. They were to be accompanied, at least as far as Isle

---

[1] Parkman's "Jesuits in North America," pp. 1, 2.

4

des Allumettes, by Nicolet on his way to the Winnebagoes.[1]

At Three Rivers, Nicolet assisted in a manner in the permanent foundation of the place, by helping to plant some of the pickets of the fort just commenced. The Hurons, assembled there for the purposes of trade, were ready to return to their homes, and with them the missionaries, as well as Nicolet, expected to journey up the Ottawa. The savages were few in number, and much difficulty was experienced in getting permits from them to carry so many white men, as other Frenchmen were also of the company. It was past the middle of July before all were on their way.

That Nicolet did not visit the Winnebagoes previous to 1634, is reasonably certain. Champlain would not, in 1632, have located upon his map Green bay north of Lake Superior, as was done by him in that year, had Nicolet been there before that date.

---

[1] This is assumed, although in no account that has been discovered is it expressly asserted that he visited the tribe just mentioned during this year. In no record, contemporaneous or later, is the date of his journey thither given, except approximately. The fact of Nicolet's having made the journey to the Winnebagoes is first noticed by Vimont, in the *Relation* of 1640, p. 35. He says: " Ie visiteray tout maintenant le costé du Sud, ie diray on passant que le sieur Nicolet, interprete en langue Algonquine et Huronne pour Messieurs de la nouuelle France, m'a donné les noms de ces nations qu'il a visitées luy mesme pour la pluspart dans leur pays, tous ces peuples entendent l'Algonquin, excepté les Hurons, qui out vne langue à part, comme aussi les Ouinipigou [*Winnebagoes*] ou gens de mer." The year of Nicolet's visit, it will be noticed, is thus left undetermined. The extract only shows that it must have been made " in or before " 1639.

As he was sent by Champlain, the latter must have had knowledge of his going; so that had he started in 1632, or the previous year, the governor would, doubtless, have awaited his return before noting down, from Indian reports only, the location of rivers and lakes and the homes of savage nations in those distant regions.

It has already been shown, that Nicolet probably returned to Quebec in 1633, relinquishing his home among the Nipissing Indians that year. And that he did not immediately set out at the command of Champlain to return up the Ottawa and journey thence to the Winnebagoes, is certain; as the savages from the west, then trading at the site of what is now Three Rivers, were in no humor to allow him to retrace his steps, even had he desired it.[1]

It may, therefore, be safely asserted that, before the year 1634, " those so remote countries," lying to the northward and northwestward, beyond the Georgian bay of Lake Huron, had never been seen by civilized man. But, did Nicolet visit those ulterior regions in 1634, returning thence in 1635? That these were the years of his explorations and discoveries, there can be no longer any doubt.[2] After the ninth day of December, of the last-mentioned year, his continued presence upon the St. Lawrence is a matter of record, up to the day of his death, except from the nineteenth of March, 1638, to the ninth of January,

---

[1] As to the temper of the Hurons at that date, see Parkman's "Jesuits in North America," p. 51.

[2] The credit of first advancing this idea is due to Benjamin Sulte. See his article entitled " Jean Nicolet," in " Mélanges D' Histoire et de Littérature," Ottawa, 1876, pp. 426, 436.

1639. These ten months could not have seen him journeying from Quebec to the center of what is now Wisconsin, and return; for, deducting those which could not have been traveled in because of ice in the rivers and lakes, and the remaining ones were too few for his voyage, considering the number of tribes he is known to have visited. Then, too, the Iroquois had penetrated the country of the Algonquins, rendering it totally unsafe for such explorations, even by a Frenchman. Besides, it may be stated that Champlain was no longer among the living, and that with him died the spirit of discovery which alone could have prompted the journey.

Furthermore, the marriage of Nicolet, which had previously taken place, militates against the idea of his having attempted any more daring excursions among savage nations. As, therefore, he certainly traveled up the Ottawa, as far as Isle des Allumettes, in 1634,[1] and as there is no evidence of his having been upon the St. Lawrence until near the close of the next year, the conclusion, from these facts alone, is irresistible that, during this period, he accomplished, as hereafter detailed, the exploration of the western countries; visited the Winnebagoes, as well as several neighboring nations, and returned to the St. Lawrence; all of which, it is believed, could not have been performed in one summer.[2] But what, heretofore, has been a very strong

---

[1] Brébeuf, *Relation des Hurons,* 1635, p. 30. He says: "Iean Nicolet, en son voyage qu'il fit auec nous iusques à l'Isle," etc.; meaning the Isle des Allumettes, in the Ottawa river.

[2] Incidents recorded in the *Relations,* and in the parish church register of Three Rivers, show Nicolet to have been upon the St. Lawrence from December 9, 1635, to his death, in 1642, except

probability, is now seen clearly to be **a fact; as it is
certainly known that** an **agreement for peace was
made some time before** June, 1635, between certain
Indian **tribes (Winnebagoes and Nez** Percés), which,
as the **account indicates, was brough tabout by Nicolet in his journey to the Far West.**[1]

during the ten months above **mentioned.** It is an unfortunate fact that, for those ten months, the record of **the** church just named is missing. For this information I am indebted to Mr. Benjamin Sulte. . Could the missing record be found, **it** would be seen to contain, without doubt, some references to Nicolet's presence at **Three Rivers.** As the *Relation* of 1640 **mentions** Nicolet's visit to the **Winnebagoes, it could not have** been made subsequent to 1639. It has **already** been shown how improbable it is that his journey was **made previous** to 1634. It only remains, therefore, **to give** his **whereabouts** previous to 1640, and subsequent **to 1635. His presence in Three** Rivers, according to Mr. **Sulte (see** Appendix, **I., to this narrative), is noted in** the parish **register in** December, **1635; in May, 1636; in November and December, 1637; in March,** 1638; **in January,** March, **July,** October, **and** December, 1639. As to mention of him in the *Relations* during those years, see the next chapter of this work.

It was the identification by **Mr.** Shea, of **the** Winnebagoes as the "Ouinipigou," or "Gens **de Mer,"** of the *Relations,* that enabled him to call the attention of the public **to** the extent of the discoveries of Nicolet. **The** claims of the latter, as the discoverer of the Northwest, were thus, for the first time, brought forward on the page of American history.

[1] " Le huictiesme **de Iuin, le Capitaine des** Naiz percez, **ou de la** Nation du Castor, qui est à **trois iournées de nous, vint nous demander** quelqu'vn de nos François, pour aller **auec eux passer** l'Este dans vn fort qu'ils ont fait, pour la crainte qu'ils ont des ASeatsi8aenrrhonon, c'est à dire, des gens puants, qui ont rompu le **traicté** de paix, et ont tuè deux de leurs dont ils ont fait festin."
—**Le Jeune,** *Relation,* 1636, p. 92.

"**On the 18th of June** [1635], the **chief of the Nez** Percés, or **Beaver Nation, which** is three days' **journey from us [the** Jesuit

The sufferings endured by all the Frenchmen, except Nicolet, in traveling up the Ottawa, were very severe. The latter had been so many years among the Indians, was so inured to the toils of the wilderness, that he met every hardship with the courage, the fortitude, and the strength of the most robust savage.[1] Not so with the rest of the party. "Barefoot, lest their shoes should injure the frail vessel, each crouched in his canoe, toiling with unpracticed hands to propel it. Before him, week after week, he saw the same lank, unkempt hair, the same tawny shoulders, and long naked arms ceaselessly plying the paddle."[2] A scanty diet of Indian-corn gave them little strength to assist in carrying canoes and baggage across the numerous portages. They were generally ill-treated by the savages, and only reached the Huron villages after great peril. Nicolet remained for a time at Isle des Allumettes, where he parted with Brébeuf.

To again meet "the Algonquins of the Isle" must have been a pleasure to Nicolet; but he could not

missionaries, located at the head of Georgian bay of Lake Huron], came to demand of us some one of our Frenchmen to go with them to pass the summer in a fort which they have made, by reason of the fear which they have of the *Aweatiswaenrrhonon;* * that is to say, of the Nation of the Puants [Winnebagoes], who have broken the treaty of peace, and have killed two of their men, of whom they have made a feast."

[1] Iean Nicolet, en son voyage qu' il fit auec nous iusques à l' Isle souffrit aussi tous les trauaux d' vn des plus robustes Sauuages.' —Brébeuf, *Relation*, 1635, p. 30.

[2] Parkman's "Jesuits in North America," p. 53.

* The figure 8 which occurs in this word in the *Relation* of 1636, is supposed to be equivalent, in English, to "w," "we," or "oo."

tarry long with them. To the Huron villages, on the borders of Georgian bay, he was to go before entering upon his journey to unexplored countries. To them he must hasten, as to them he was first accredited by Champlain. He had a long distance to travel from the homes of that nation before reaching the Winnebagoes. There was need, therefore, for expedition. He must yet make his way up the Ottawa to the Mattawan, a tributary, and by means of the latter reach Lake Nipissing. Thence, he would float down French river to Georgian bay.[1] And, even after this body of water was reached, it would require a considerable canoe navigation, coasting along to the southward, before he could set foot upon Huron territory. So Nicolet departed from the Algonquins of the Isle, and arrived safely at the Huron towns.[2] Was he a stranger to this nation? Had he, during his long sojourn among the Nipissings, visited their villages? Certain it is he could speak their language. He must have had, while residing with the Algonquins, very frequent intercourse with Huron parties, who often visited Lake Nipissing and the Ottawa

---

[1] The Mattawan has its source on the very verge of Lake Nipissing, so that it was easy to make a "portage" there to reach the lake. The Indians, and afterward the French, passed by the Mattawan, Mattouane, or Mattawin ("the residence of the beaver"), went over the small space of land called the "portage," that exists between the two waters, floated on Lake Nipissing, and followed the French river, which flows directly out of that lake to the Georgian bay.

A "portage" is a place, as is well known, where parties had to "port" their baggage in order to reach the next navigable water.

[2] Vimont, *Relation*, 1643, p. 3.

river for purposes of trade.¹ But why was Nicolet accredited by Champlain to the Hurons at all? Was not the St. Lawrence visited yearly by their traders? It could not have been, therefore, to establish a commerce with them. Neither could it have been to explore their country; for the *voyageur*, the fur-trader, the missionary, even Champlain himself, as we have seen, had already been at their towns. Was the refusal, a year previous, of their trading-parties at Quebec to take the Jesuits to their homes the cause of Nicolet's being sent to smoke the pipe of peace with their chiefs? This could not have been the reason, else the missionaries would not have preceded him from the Isle des Allumettes. He certainly had to travel many miles out of his way in going from the Ottawa to the Winnebagoes by way of the Huron villages. His object was, evidently, to inform the Hurons that the governor of Canada was anxious to have amicable relations established between them and the Winnebagoes, and to obtain a few of the nation to accompany him upon his mission of peace.²

---

[1] "Sieur Nicolet, interpreter en langue Algonquine et Huronne," etc.—Vimont, *Relation*, 1640, p. 35.

The Hurons and Nipissings were, at that date, great friends, having constant intercourse, according to all accounts of those days.

[2] "The People of the Sea"—that is, the Winnebagoes—were frequently at war with the Hurons, Nez Percés, and other nations on the Georgian bay, which fact was well known to the governor of Canada. Now, the good offices of Nicolet were to be interposed to bring about a reconciliation between these nations. He, it is believed, was also to carry out Champlain's policy of making the Indian tribes the allies of the French. Vimont (*Relation*, 1643, p. 3) says, he was chosen to make a journey to the Winne-

NICOLET DISCOVERS THE NORTHWEST.   49

It was now that Nicolet, after all ceremonies and
"talks" with the Hurons were ended, began preparations for his voyage to the Winnebagoes. He was
to strike boldly into undiscovered regions. He was
to encounter savage **nations never** before visited. It
was, in reality, the beginning of a voyage full of dangers—one that would require great **tact, great** courage, and constant facing of difficulties. No one,
however, understood better the savage character than
he; no Frenchman was more fertile of resources.
From the St. Lawrence, he had brought presents to
conciliate the Indian tribes which he would meet.
Seven Hurons were to accompany him.[1] Before him lay
great lakes; around him, when on land, would frown
dark forests. A birch-bark canoe was to bear the first
white man along the northern shore of Lake Huron,
and upon Saint Mary's strait[2] to the falls—"**Sault
Sainte Marie;**" many miles on Lake Michigan; thence,
up Green bay to the homes of the Winnebagoes:[3] and

bagoes and treat for peace with them *and with the Hurons;* show-
ing, it is suggested, that it was not only to bring about a peace
between the two tribes, but to attach them both to French interests.
The **words of** Vimont are these:

"**Pendant qu'il exerçoit cette** charge, il [*Nicolet*] fut delegué
pour **faire vn voyage en la** nation appelleé des Gens de Mer, et
traitter la paix auec **eux et les** Hurons, desquels il sont esloignés,
tirant, vers l'Oüest, d'enuiron **trois** cents lieuës."

[1] "I'l [*Nicolet*] s'embarque au pays des Hurons auec sept Sauuages."—Vimont, *Relation,* 1643, p. 3.

[2] Saint Mary's strait separates the Dominion of Canada from
the upper peninsula of Michigan, and connects Lake Superior
with Lake Huron.

[3] The route taken by Nicolet, from the mouth of French river,

that canoe was to lead the van of a mighty fleet indeed, as the commerce of the upper lakes can testify. With him, he had a number of presents.

What nations were encountered by him on the way to "the People of the Sea," from the Huron villages? Three—all of Algonquin lineage—occupied the shores of the Georgian bay, before the mouth of French river had been reached. Concerning them, little is known, except their names.[1] Passing the river which flows from Lake Nipissing, Nicolet "upon the same shores of this fresh-water sea," that is, upon the shores of Lake Huron, came next to "the Nation of Beavers,"[2] whose hunting-grounds were northward of the Manitoulin islands.[3] This nation

---

in journeying toward the Winnebagoes, is sufficiently indicated by (1) noting that, in mentioning the various tribes visited by him, Nicolet probably gave their names, except the Ottawas, in the order in which he met them; and (2) by calculating his time as more limited on his return than on his outward trip, because of his desire to descend the Ottawa with the annual flotilla of Huron canoes, which would reach the St. Lawrence in July, 1635.

[1] The Ouasouarim, the Outchougai, and the Atchiligouan.— Vimont, *Relation*, 1640, p. 34.

[2] Called Amikoüai (*Rel.*, 1640, p. 34), from *Amik* or *Amikou*—a beaver.

[3] The Manitoulin islands stretch from east to west along the north shores of Lake Huron, and consist chiefly of the Great Manitoulin or Sacred Isle, Little Manitoulin or Cockburn, and Drummond. Great Manitoulin is eighty miles long by twenty broad. Little Manitoulin has a diameter of about seven miles. Drummond is twenty-four miles long, with a breadth varying from two to twelve miles. It is separated from the American shore, on the west, by a strait called the True Detour, which is scarcely one mile wide, and forms the principal passage for vessels proceeding to Lake Superior.

was afterward esteemed among the most noble of those of Canada. They were supposed to be descended from the Great Beaver, which was, next to the Great Hare, their principal divinity. They inhabited originally the Beaver islands, in Lake Michigan; afterward the Manitoulin islands; then they removed to the main-land, where they were found by Nicolet. Farther on, but still upon the margin of the great lake, was found another tribe.[1] This people, and the Amikoüai, were of the Algonquin family, and their language was not difficult to be understood by Nicolet. Entering, finally, St. Mary's strait, his canoes were urged onward for a number of miles, until the falls—Sault de Sainte Marie[2]—were reached: and there stood Nicolet, the first white man to set foot upon any portion of what was, more than a century and a half after, called "the territory northwest of the river Ohio,"[3] now the States of Ohio, Indiana, Il-

---

[1] The Oumisagai.—Vimont, *Relation*, 1640, p. 34.

[2] These falls are distinctly marked on Champlain's map of 1632; and on that of Du Creux of 1660.

[3] In giving Nicolet this credit, it is necessary to state, that the governor of Canada, in 1688, claimed that honor for Champlain (N. Y. Col. Doc., Vol. IX., p. 378). He says:

"In the years 1611 and 1612, he [Champlain] ascended the Grand river [Ottawa] as far as Lake Huron, called the Fresh sea [La Mer Douce]; he went thence to the Petun [Tobacco] Nation, next to the Neutral Nation and to the Macoutins [Mascoutins], who were then residing near the place called the Sakiman [that part of the present State of Michigan lying between the head of Lake Erie and Saginaw bay, on Lake Huron]; from that he went to the Algonquin and Huron tribes, at war against the Iroquois [Five Nations]. He passed by places he has, himself, described in his book [Les Voyages De La Novvelle France, etc., 1632], which are no other than Detroit [*i. e.*, "the straight," now

linois, Michigan, and Wisconsin, and so much of
Minnesota as lies east of the Mississippi river.

called Detroit river] and Lake Erie."—*Mem. of M. de Denonville,
May* 8, 1688.

The reader is referred to Champlain's Map of 1632, and to "his
book" of the same date, for a complete refutation of the assertion as to his visiting, at any time before that year, the
Mascoutins. In 1632, Champlain, as shown by his map of that
year, had no knowledge whatever of Lake Erie or Lake St.
Clair, nor had he previously been so far west as Detroit river.
It is, of course, well known, that he did not go west of the
St. Lawrence during that year or subsequent to that date. Locating the Mascoutins "near the place called the Sakiman," is as
erroneous as that Champlain ever visited those savages. The
reported distance between him when at the most westerly point
of his journeyings and the Mascoutins is shown by himself:
"After having visited these people [the Tobacco Nation, in December, 1615] we left the place and came to a nation of Indians
which we have named the Standing Hair [Ottawas], who were
very much rejoiced to see us again [he had met them previously
on the Ottawa river], with whom also we formed a friendship,
and who, in like manner, promised to come and find us and see
us at the said habitation. At this place it seems to me appropriate to give a description of their country, manners, and modes
of action. In the first place, they make war upon another nation
of Indians, called the Assistagueronon, which means nation of
fire [Mascoutins], ten days distant from them."—*Voyages*, 1632,
I., p. 262 [272].

Upon his map of 1632, Champlain speaks of the "discoveries"
made by him "in the year 1614 and 1615, until in the year 1618"
—" of this great lake [Huron], and of all the lands *from the Sau't
St. Louis* [the rapids in the St. Lawrence];"— but he nowhere
intimates that he had made discoveries *west* of that lake. It is,
therefore, certain that the first white man who ever saw or explored any portion of the territory forming the present State of
Michigan was John Nicolet—not Champlain. Compare Parkman's " Pioneers of France in the New World," Chap. XIV., and
map illustrative of the text.

Among "the People of the Falls,"[1] at their principal village, on the south side of the strait, at the foot of the rapids,[2] in what is now the State of Michigan,[3] Nicolet and his **seven** Hurons rested from the fatigues **of** their weary voyage.[4] They were still with Algonquins.

---

[1] **Their name, as** stated by Nicolet and preserved in **the** *Relation* **of 1640,** was Baouichtigouin; given in the *Relation* **of** 1642, as Paüoitigoüeieuhak—"inhabitants of the falls;" in the *Relation* **of** 1648, as Paouitagoung—"nation of the Sault;" on Du Creux' map of 1660, " PasitigSecü;" and they were sometimes known as Paouitingouach-irini—"the men of the shallow cataract." They were estimated, **in** 1671, **at one hundred and** fifty **souls.** They then united **with** other **kindred nations.**
By the **French, these tribes,** collectively, were called Sauteurs; but they were **known to the** Iroquois as Estiaghicks, or Stiagigroone—**the termination,** *roone,* meaning men, being applied to In**dians** of the **Algonquin** family. They were designated by **the Sioux as** Raratwaus or "people of the falls." They **were** the ancestors **of** the modern Otchipwes, **or** Ojibwas (Chippewas).

[2] That this was the location in **1641** is certain. Shea's *Catholic Missions,* p. 184. In 1669, it was, probably, still at the foot of the rapids, on the southern side. *Id.,* p. 361. Besides, when the missionaries first visited the Sault, they were informed that the place had been occupied for a long period. The falls are correctly marked upon Champlain's map of 1632.

[3] **The** earliest delineation, to any extent, of the present State **of Michigan, is that to** be found on **Du** Creux' Map of 1660, **where** the two peninsulas are very well represented in outline.

[4] The names of the tribes thus **far visited** by Nicolet, and their relative positions, are shown in the **following** from Vimont (*Relation,* 1640, p. 34), except that the "cheueux releucz" were not called upon by him until his return:

" I'ay dit qu'à l'entrée du premier de ces Lacs se rencontrent les Hurons; les quittans pour voguer plus haut dans le lac, on truue au Nord les Ouasouarim, plus haut sont les Outchougai, plus haut encore à l'embouchure du fleuue qui vient du Lac Nipisin sont les Atchiligoüan. **Au** delà sur les mesmes riues de ceste mer

From Lake Huron they had entered upon one of the channels of the magnificent water-way leading out from Lake Superior, and threaded their way, now through narrow rapids, now across (as it were) little lakes, now around beautiful islands, to within fifteen miles of the largest expanse of fresh water on the globe—stretching away in its grandeur to the westward, a distance of full four hundred miles.[1] Nicolet saw beyond him the falls; around him clusters of wigwams, which two centuries and a half have changed into public buildings and private residences, into churches and warehouses, into offices and stores—in short, into a pleasantly-situated American village,[2] frequently visited by steamboats carrying valuable freight and crowded with parties of pleasure. The portage around the falls, where, in early times, the Indian carried his birch-bark canoe, has given place to an excellent canal. Such are the changes which "the course of empire" continually

---

douce sont les Amikoüai, ou la nation du Castor, au Sud desquels est vne Isle dans ceste mer douce longue d'enuiron trente lieuës habitée des Outaouan, ce sont peuples venus de la nation des cheueux releuez. Apres les Amikouai sur les mesmes riues du grand lac sont les Oumisagai, qu'on passe pour venir à Baouichtigouin, c'est à dire, à la nation des gens du Sault, pource qu'en effect il y a vn Sault qui se iette en cet endroit dans la mer douce."

[1] Lake Superior is distinctly marked on Champlain's map of 1632, where it appears as "Grand Lac." Was it seen by Nicolet? This is a question which will probably never be answered to the satisfaction of the historian.

[2] Sault Sainte Marie (pronounced *soo-saint-máry*), county-seat of Chippewa county, Michigan, fifteen miles below the outlet of Lake Superior.

brings to view in "the vast, illimitable, changing west."

Nicolet tarried among "the People of the Falls," probably, but a brief period. His voyage, after leaving them, must have been to him one of great interest. He returned down the strait, passing, it is thought, through the western "detour" to Mackinaw.[1] Not very many miles brought him to "the second fresh-water sea," Lake Michigan.[2] He is fairly entitled to the honor of its discovery; for no white man had ever before looked out upon its broad expanse. Nicolet was soon gliding along upon the clear waters of this out-of-the-way link in the great chain of lakes. The bold Frenchman fearlessly threaded his way along its northern shore, frequently stopping upon what is now known as "the upper peninsula" of Michigan, until the bay of Noquet[3]

---

[1] The Straits of Mackinaw connect Lake Michigan with Lake Huron. Of the word "Mackinaw," there are many synonyms to be found upon the pages of American history: Mackinac, Michillmakinaw, Michillimakinac, Michilimakina, Michiliakimawk, Michilinaaquina, Miscilemackina, Miselimackinack, Misilemakinak, Missilimakina, Missilimakinac, Missilimakinak, Missilimaquina, Missilimaquinak, etc.

[2] Machihiganing was the Indian name; called by the French at an early day, Mitchiganon,—sometimes the Lake of the Illinois, Lake St. Joseph, or Lake Dauphin. I know of no earlier representation of this lake than that on Du Creux' map of 1660. It is there named the "Magnus Lacus Algonquinorum, seu Lacus Foetetium [Foetentium]." This is equivalent to Great Algonquin Lake, or Lake of the Puants; that is, Winnebago Lake. On a map by Joliet, recently published by Gabriel Gravier, it is called " Lac des Illinois ou Missihiganin."

[3] Bay du Noquet, or Noque. That the "small lake" visited by Nicolet was, in fact, this bay, is rendered probable by the phrase-

was reached, which is, in reality, a northern arm of Green bay.¹ Here, upon its northern border, he visited another Algonquin tribe;² also one living to the northward of this "small lake."³ These tribes never navigated those waters any great distance, but lived upon the fruits of the earth.⁴ Making his way up Green bay, he finally reached the Menomonee river, its principal northern affluent.⁵

---

ology employed by Vimont in the *Relation* of 1640, p. 35. He says: "Passing this small lake [from the Sault Sainte Marie], we enter into the second fresh-water sea [Lake Michigan and Green bay]." It is true Vimont speaks of "the small lake" as lying "beyond the falls;" but his meaning is, "nearer the Winnebagoes." If taken literally, his words would indicate a lake further up the strait, above the Sault Sainte Marie, meaning Lake Superior, which, of course, would not answer the description of a small lake. It must be remembered that the missionary was writing at his home upon the St. Lawrence, and was giving his description from his standpoint.

¹ Synonyms: La Baye des Eaux Puantes, La Baye, Enitajghe (Iroquois), Baie des Puants, La Grande Baie, Bay des Puants.

² Called the Roquai, by Vimont, in the *Relation* of 1640, p. 34—probably the Noquets—afterwards classed with the Chippewas.

³ Called the Mantoue in the *Relation* just cited. They were probably the Nantoue of the *Relation* of 1671, or Mantoueouee of the map attached thereto. They are mentioned, at that date, as living near the Foxes. In the *Relation* of 1673, they are designated as the Makoueoue, still residing near the Foxes.

⁴ "Au delà de ce Sault on trouue le petit lac, sur les bords duquel du costé du Nord sont les Roquai. Au Nord de ceux-cy sont Mantoue, ces peuples ne nauigent guiere, viuans des fruicts de la terre."—Vimont, *Relation*, 1640, pp. 34, 35.

⁵ The Menomonee river forms a part of the northeastern boundary of Wisconsin, running in a southeasterly direction between this state and Michigan, and emptying into Green bay on the northwest side. The earliest location, on a map, of a

NICOLET DISCOVERS THE NORTHWEST.

In the valley of the Menomonee, **Nicolet met a populous tribe of Indians—the Menomonees.**[1] To his surprise, no doubt, he **found they were of a lighter complexion than any other savages he had ever seen.** Their language was difficult to **understand, yet it showed** the nation to be of the Algonquin stock. Their **food was** largely **of wild rice,** which **grew** in great **abundance** in their country. They were adepts in fishing, **and** hunted, with skill, the game which abounded in the forests. They had their homes and hunting grounds upon **the** stream which still bears their name.[2]

Nicolet soon resumed his journey toward the Winnebagoes, who had already been made aware of his near approach ; for he had sent forward one of his

---

Menomonee **village, is that given** by Charlevoix **on his "Carte des Lacs du Canada,"** accompanying his **" Histoire et Description** Generale de **la Nouvelle France," Vol. I.,** Paris, **1744. The village ("des Malonines")** is placed at the mouth **of the river, on** what **is now** the Michigan side of the **stream.**

[1] Synonyms: Maroumine, Oumalouminek, Oumaominiecs, Malhominies,—meaning, in Algonquin, wild rice (*Zizania aquatica* of Linnæus). The French called this grain wild oats—folles avoine; hence they **gave** the **name of** Les Folles Avoine **to** the **Menomonees.**

" Passant ce plus **petit** lac, on entre dans la seconde mer douce, sur les riues de **laquelle sont les** Maroumine."—Vimont, *Relation,* 1640, p. 35.

[2] **I have drawn,** for this description **of the** Menomonees, upon the earliest accounts preserved **of them; but these** are of dates some years subsequent to Nicolet's **visit.** (Compare Marquette's **account in his** published narrative, by Shea.) Vimont seems not to have derived any knowledge of them from Nicolet, beside the **simple fact of** his having visited them ; at least, he says nothing **further in the *Relation* of** 1640.

Hurons to carry the news of his coming and of his mission of peace. The messenger and his message were well received. The Winnebagoes dispatched several of their young men to meet the "wonderful man." They go to him—they escort him—they carry his baggage.¹ He was clothed in a large garment of Chinese damask, sprinkled with flowers and birds of different colors.² But, why thus attired? Possibly,

---

¹ "Two days' journey from this tribe [the Winnebagoes], he sent one of his savages," etc.—Vimont, *Relation*, 1643, p. 3. This was just the distance from the Menomonees. Du Creux, although following the *Relation* of 1643, makes Nicolet an ambassador of the Hurons, for he says (Hist. Canada, p. 360): "When he [Nicolet] was two days distant [from the Winnebagoes], he sent forward one of his own company to make known to the nation to which they were going, that a European ambassador was approaching with gifts, who, in behalf of the Hurons, desired to secure their friendship." But the following is the account of Vimont (*Relation*, 1643, p. 3), from the time of Nicolet's departure from the Huron villages to his being met by the young men of the Winnebagoes:

"Ils [*Nicolet and his seven Hurons*] passerent par quantité de petites nations, en allant et en reuenant; lors qu'ils y arriuoient, ils fichoient deux bastons en terre, auquel ils pendoient des presens, afin d'oster à ces peuples la pensée de les prendre pour ennemis et de les massacrer. A deux iournées de cette nation, il enuoya vn de ces Sauuages porter la nouuelle de la paix, laquelle fut bien receuë, nommément quand on entendit que c'estoit vn European qui portoit la parole. On depescha plusieurs ieunes gens pour aller au deuant du Manitouiriniou, c'est à dire de l'homme merueilleux ; on y vient on le conduit, on porte tout son bagage."

² Compare Parkman's "Discovery of the Great West," p. xx. "Il [*Nicolet*] estoit reuestu d'vne grande robe de damas de la Chine, toute parsemée de fleurs et d'oyseaux de diuerses couleurs."—Vimont, *Relation*, 1643, p. 3.

he had reached the far east; he was, really, in what is now the State of Wisconsin.[1] Possibly, a party of mandarins would soon greet him and welcome him to Cathay. And this robe—this dress of ceremony—was brought all the way from Quebec, doubtless, with

---

[1] **Wisconsin takes its** name from its principal river, which **drains an** extensive portion of its surface. It rises in Lake Vieux Desert (which is partly in Michigan and partly in Wisconsin), flows generally a south course to Portage, in what is now Columbia county, where it turns to the southwest, and, after a further course of one hundred and eighteen miles, with a rapid current, reaches the Mississippi river, four miles below Prairie du Chien. Its entire length is about four **hundred and fifty** miles, descending, in that distance, a **little more than** one thousand feet. Along the lower portion **of** the stream are the high lands or river hills. Some of these hills **present** high and precipitous faces towards **the water.** Others terminate in knobs. The name is supposed **to** have **been taken** from this feature; **the word** being derived from *mis-si*, great, and **os-sin,** a stone **or** rock.

Compare Shea's *Discovery and Exploration of the Mississippi*, pp. 6 (note) and 268; Foster's *Mississippi Valley*, p. 2 (note); Schoolcraft's *Thirty Years with the Indian Tribes*, p. 220 and note.

Two definitions of the word are current—as widely differing from each other as from the one just given. (See Wis. Hist. Soc. **Coll.,** Vol. I., p. 111, and Webster's Dic., Unabridged, p. 1632.) The first—"the gathering of the waters"—has no corresponding **words in** Algonquin at all resembling the name; the same may be said of the second—"wild rushing channel." (See Otchipwe Dic. of **Rev. F.** Baraga.)

Since first used by the French, the word "Wisconsin" has undergone considerable change. On the map by Joliet, recently brought to light by Gravier, it **is** given **as** "Miskonsing." In Marquette's journal, published by Thevenot, in Paris, 1681, it is noted as the "Meskousing." It appeared there for the first time in print. Hennepin, in 1683, wrote "Onisconsin" and "Misconsin;" Charlevoix, 1743, "Ouisconsing;" Carver, 1766, "Ouisconsin" (English—"Wisconsin"):since which last mentioned date, the orthography **has been** uniform.

a view to such contingency. As soon as he came in sight, all the women and children fled, seeing a man carrying thunder in his two hands; for thus it was they called his pistols, which he discharged on his right and on his left.[1] He was a manito! Nicolet's journey was, for the present, at an end. He and his Huron's "rested from their labors," among the Winnebagoes,[2] who were located around the head of Green bay,[3] contiguous to the point where it re-

---

[1] "Si tost qu'on l'apperceut toutes les femmes et les enfans s'enfuïrent, voyant vn homme porter le tonnerre en ses deux mains (c'est ainsi qu'ils nommoient deux pistolets qu'il tenoit)."—Vimont, *Relation*, 1643, p. 3.

Du Creux (Hist. Canada, p. 360) has this rendering of Vimont's language: "He [Nicolet] carried in each hand a small pistol. When he had discharged these (for he must have done this, though the French author does not mention the fact), the more timid persons, boys and women, betook themselves to flight, to escape as quickly as possible from a man who (they said) carried the thunder in both his hands." And thus Parkman ("Discovery of the Great West," p. xx.): "[Nicolet] advanced to meet the expectant crowd with a pistol in each hand. The squaws and children fled, screaming that it was a manito, or spirit, armed with thunder and lightning."

[2] Synonyms: Ouinipigou, Ouinbegouc, Ouinipegouc, Ouenibegoutz—Gens de Mer, Gens de Eaux de Mer—Des Puans, Des Puants, La Nation des Puans, La Nation des Puants, Des Gens Puants.

By the Hurons, this nation was known as A8catsi8aenrrhonon (*Relation*, 1636, p. 92); by the Sioux, as Ontonkah; but they called themselves Otchagras, Hochungara, Ochungarand, or Horoji.

[3] Champlain's map of 1632 gives them that location. La Jeune (*Relation*, 1639, p. 55) approximates their locality thus:

 . . . "Nous auons aussi pensé d'appliquer quelques-vns á la connoissance de nouuelles langues. Nous iettions les yeux sur trois autres des Peuples plus voisins: sur celle des Algonquains,

ceives the waters of **Fox river.**[1] Nicolet found the Winnebagoes **a numerous and** sedentary peo-

espars **de tous costez, et au** Midy, **et au** Septentrion de **nostre grand Lac; sur celle de la Nation** neutre, qui est vne maistresse **porte pour les païs meridionaux, et sur celle de la** Nation des **Puants, qui est vn passage des plus considerables** pour les païs **Occidentaux, vn** peu plus Septentrionaux."

"**We** [the missionaries] have also thought of applying ourselves, some of us, to the task of acquiring a knowledge of new languages. We turn our eyes on three other nations nearer: on that of the Algonquins, scattered on every side, both to the south and north of our great lake [Huron]; on that of the Neuter nation, which affords a principal entrance to **the** countries on south; **and on that of** the nation of **the** Puants [Winnebagoes], which is **one of the more** important thoroughfares to the western **countries, a little more** northern."

[1] **Fox river heads in the** northeastern **part** of Columbia county, Wisconsin, **and in** the adjoining **portions of Green** Lake county. Flowing, at first, southwest and then **due west, it approaches the** Wisconsin **at Portage, county-seat of Columbia county. When** within less **than two miles of that river, separated from it by** only a low, sandy plain—the famous "portage" of **early** days— it turns abruptly northward, and **with a** sluggish current, con**tinues on** this course, for twelve miles, to the head of Lake Buffalo, **in the** southern part of which is now Marquette county, Wisconsin. It now begins a wide curve, which brings its direction finally around due east. Lake Buffalo is merely an expansion of the river, thirteen and one-half miles long and half a mile **wide. From** the foot of this lake, the river runs in **an** irregular, **easterly** course, **with a somewhat** rapid current, to **the** head of Puckaway lake, which is eight and one-fourth miles in length, and from **one to two** miles wide. **At** the foot of this lake there are wide marshes through which the river leaves on the north side, and, after making a long, narrow bend to **the** west, begins a northeast stretch, which it continues for a considerable distance, passing, after receiving the waters of Wolf river, around in **a** curve to the southeast through Big Butte Des Morts

ple,[1] speaking a language radically different from any of the Algonquin nations, as well as from the Hurons.[2] They were of the Dakota stock.[3] The news of the Frenchman's coming spread through the country. Four or five thousand people assembled of different tribes.[4] Each of the chiefs gave a ban-

---

lake, and reaching Lake Winnebago, into which it flows at the city of Oshkosh.

The river leaves Winnebago lake in two channels, at the cities of Menasha and Neenah, flowing in a westerly course to the Little Butte Des Morts lake, and through the latter in a north course, when it soon takes a northeasterly direction, which it holds until it empties into the head of Green bay. The stream gets its name from the Fox tribe of Indians formerly residing in its valley. Upon Champlain's map of 1632, it is noted as "Riviere des Puans;" that is, "River of the Puans"—Winnebago river. The name Neenah (water), sometimes applied to it, is a misnomer.

[1] "Plus auant encore sur les mesmes riues habitent les Ouinipigou [Winnebagoes], peuples sedentaires qui sont en grand nombre."—Vimont, *Relation*, 1640, p. 35.

[2] "Tous ces peuples entendent l'Algonquin, excepté les Hurons, qui ont vne langue à part, comme aussi les Ouinipigou [Winnebagoes] ou gens de mer."—Ibid.

[3] The Winnebagoes and some bands of Sioux were the only Dakotas that crossed the Mississippi in their migratory movement eastward.

[4] Says Vimont (*Relation*, 1643, pp. 3, 4): "La nouuelle de sa venuë s'espandit incontinent aux lieu circonuoisins: il se fit vne assemblée, de quartre ou cinq mille hommes."

But this number is lessened somewhat by the *Relation* of 1656 (p. 39):

"Vn François m'a dit autrefois, qu'il auoit veu trois mille hommes dans vne assemblée qui se fit pour traiter de paix, au Païs des gens de Mer."

"A Frenchman [Nicolet] told me some time ago, that he had seen three thousand men together in one assemblage, for the

quet. One of the sachems regaled his guests with at least one hundred and twenty beavers.¹ The large assemblage was prolific of speeches and ceremonies. Nicolet did not fail to "speak of peace" upon that interesting occasion.² He urged upon the nation the advantages of an alliance, rather than war, with the nations to the eastward of Lake Huron. They agreed to keep the peace with the Hurons, Nez Percés, and, possibly, other tribes; but, soon after Nicolet's return, they sent out war parties against the Beaver nation. Doubtless the advantages of trade with the colony upon the St. Lawrence were depicted in glowing colors by the Frenchman. But the courageous Norman was not satisfied with a visit to the Winnebagoes only. He must see the neighboring tribes. So he ascended the Fox river of Green bay to Winnebago lake—passing through which, he again entered that stream, paddling his canoe up its current, until he reached the homes of the Mascoutins,³ the first tribe

---

purpose of making a treaty of peace in the country of the People of the Sea [Winnebagoes]."

¹ "Chacun des principaux fit son festin, en l'vn desquels on seruit au moins six-vingts Castors."—Vimont, *Relation*, 1643, p. 4.

² Shea ("Discovery and Exploration of the Mississippi Valley," p. 20) has evidently caught the true idea of Nicolet's mission to the Winnebagoes. He says: "With these [Winnebagoes] Nicolet entered into friendly relations."

³ Synonyms: Mascoutens, **Maskoutens**, Maskouteins, Musquetens, Machkoutens, Maskoutench, etc. They were called by the French, "Les Gens de Feu"—the Nation of Fire; by the Hurons, "Assistagueronons" or "Atsistaehronons," from *assista*, fire and *ronons*, people; that is, Fire-People or Fire-Nation. By Champlain, they were noted, in 1632, as "Les Gens de Feu a Bistaguer-

to be met with after leaving the Winnebagoes; for the Sacs[1] and Foxes[2] were not residents of what is now Wisconsin at that period,—their migration thither, from the east, having been at a subsequent date. Nicolet had navigated the Fox river, a six-days' journey, since leaving the Winnebagoes.[3]

---

onons" on his map. This is a misprint for "Assistagueronons," as his "Voyages" of that year shows. I., p. 262 [272].

"The Fire Nation bears this name erroneously, calling themselves Maskoutench, which signifies 'a land bare of trees,' such as that which these people inhabit; but because by the change of a few letters, the same word signifies, 'fire,' from thence it has come that they are called the 'Fire Nation.'"—*Relation*, 1671, p. 45.

[1] Synonyms: Sauks, Saukis, Ousakis, Sakys, etc.

[2] Synonyms: Outagamis, Les Renards, Musquakies.

[3] The distance by days up the Fox river of Green bay from the Winnebagoes to the Mascoutins, is given in accordance with the earliest accounts of canoe navigation upon that stream. The first white persons to pass up the river after Nicolet were Allouez and his attendants, in April, 1670. That missionary (*Relation*, 1670, pp. 96, 97, 99), says:

"The 16th of April [1670], I embarked to go and commence the mission of the Outagamis [Fox Indians], a people well known in all these parts. We were lying at the head of the bay [Green bay], at the entrance of the River of the Puants [Fox river], which we have named 'St. Francis;' in passing, we saw clouds of swans, bustards, and ducks; the savages take them in nets at the head of the bay, where they catch as many as fifty in a night; this game, in the autumn, seek the wild rice that the wind has shaken off in the month of September.

"The 17th [of April of the same year], we went up the River St. Francis [the Fox]—two and sometimes three arpens wide. After having advanced four leagues, we found the village of the savages named Saky [Sacs, Saukis, or Sauks], who began a work that merits well here to have its place. From one side of the river to the other, they made a barricade, planting great stakes,

NICOLET DISCOVERS THE NORTHWEST. 65

The Mascoutins, as we have seen, were heard of by Champlain as early as 1615, as being engaged in a war with the Neuter nation and the Ottawas. But, two fathoms from the water, in such a manner that there is, as it were, a bridge above for the fishers, who, by the aid of a little bow-net, easily take sturgeons and all other kinds of fish which this pier stops, although the water does not cease to flow between the stakes. They call this device Mitihikan ["Mitchiganen" or "Machihiganing," now "Michigan"]; they make use of it in the spring and a part of the summer.

"The 18th [of the same month], we made the portage which they call Kekaling [afterwards variously spelled, and pronounced "Cock-o-lin;" meaning, it is said, the place of the fish. In the fall of 1851, a village was laid out there, which is known as Kaukauna]; our sailors drew the canoe through the rapids; I walked on the bank of the river, where I found apple-trees and vine stocks [grape vines] in abundance.

"The 19th [April], our sailors ascended the rapids, by using poles, for two leagues. I went by land as far as the other portage, which they call Oukocitiming; that is to say, the highway. We observed this same day the eclipse of the sun, predicted by the astrologers, which lasted from mid-day until two o'clock. The third, or near it, of the body of the sun appeared eclipsed; the other two-thirds formed a crescent. We arrived, in the evening, at the entrance of the Lake of the Puants [Winnebago lake], which we have called Lake St. Francis; it is about twelve leagues long and four wide; it is situated from north-northeast to south-southwest; it abounds in fish, but uninhabited, on account of the Nardoüecis [Sioux], who are here dreaded.

"The 20th [of April, 1670], which was on Sunday, I said mass, after having navigated five or six leagues in the lake; after which, we arrived in a river [the Fox, at what is now Oshkosh], that comes from a lake of wild rice [Big Butte Des Morts lake], which we came into; at the foot [head] of which we found the river [the Wolf] which leads to the Outagamis [Fox Indians] on one side, and that [the Fox] which leads to the **Machkoutenck**

6

up to the time of Nicolet's visit, and for a number of years subsequent (as he gave no clue himself to their locality), they were only known as living two hundred leagues or more beyond the last mentioned tribe—that is, that distance beyond the south end of the Georgian bay of Lake Huron.[1] Their villages were in the valley of the Fox river, probably in what

---

[Mascoutins] on the other. We entered into the former [the Wolf]. . . .

"The 29th [of April of the same year, having returned from the Fox Indians living up the Wolf river], we entered into the [Fox] river, which leads to the Machkoutench [Mascoutins], called Assista Ectaeronnons, Fire Nation ["Gens de Feu"], by the Hurons. This [Fox] river is very beautiful, without rapids or portages [above the mouth of the Wolf]; it flows to [from] the southwest.

"The 30th [of April, 1670], having disembarked opposite the village [of the Mascoutins], and left our canoe at the water's edge, after a walk of a league, over beautiful prairies, we perceived the fort [of the Mascoutins]."

[1] Champlain's "Les Voyages de la Novvelle France," I., p. 262 [272], previously cited. Upon Champlain's Map of 1632, they are located beyond and to the south of Lake Huron, he having no knowledge of Lake Michigan. In his "Voyages," his words are: "Ils [the Cheveux Relevés—Ottawas] sont la guerre, à vne autre nation de Sauuages, qui s'appellent Assistagueronon, qui veut dire gens de feu, esloignez d'eux de dix iournées." Sagard, in 1636 ("Histoire du Canada," p. 201), is equally indefinite as to locality, though placing them westward of the south end of the Georgian bay of Lake Huron, "nine or ten days' journey by canoe, which makes about two hundred leagues, or more." He says: "Tous essemble [the different bands of the Ottowas] sont la guerre a une autre nation nommée Assistagueronon, qui veut dire gens feu : car en langue Huronne Assista signifie de feu and Eronon signifie Nation. Ils sont esloignez d'eux à ce qu'on tient, de neuf ou dix iournées de Canots, qui sont enuiron deux cens lieuës et plus de chemin."

is now Green Lake county, Wisconsin.[1] They had, doubtless, for their neighbors, the Miamis[2] and Kickapoos.[3] They were a vigorous and warlike nation, of Algonquin stock, as were also the two tribes last mentioned. Nicolet, while among the Mascoutins, heard of the Wisconsin river, which was distant only three days' journey up the tortuous channel of the Fox. But the accounts given him of that tributary of the Mississippi were evidently very confused. A reference to the parent stream (confounded with the Wisconsin) as "the great water,"[4] by the savages, caused him to believe that he was, in reality, but three days' journey from the sea; and so he reported after his return to the St. Lawrence.[5] Strange to say, Nicolet resolved not to visit this ocean, although, as he believed, so near its shores.

He traveled no further upon the Fox river,[6] but

---

[1] Allouez (*Relation*, 1670, p 99, before cited) is the first to give their position with any degree of certainty. Unless, under the name of " Rasaoua koueton," the Mascoutins were not mentioned by Nicolet, in the list given to Vimont (*Relation*, 1640, p. 35). The " R " should, probably, have been "M," thus: " Masaoua koueton."

[2] Synonyms: Miamees, Miramis, Myamicks, Omianicks, Ommiamies, Oumis, Oumiamies, Oumiamiwek, Oumamis, Twightwees. As to their place of abode, see Shea's *Hennepin*, p. 258.

[3] Synonyms: Kikabou, Kikapou, Quicapou, Kickapoux, Kickapous, Kikapoux, Quicapouz, etc.

[4] The name of this river is from the Algonquin *missi*, great, and *sepe*, water, or river. The popular notion that it means "the father of waters," is erroneous.

[5] " Le Sieur Nicolet qui a le plus auant penetré dedans ces pays si esloignés m'a asseuré que s'il eust vogué trois iours plus auant sur vn grand fleuue qui sort de ce lac, qu'il auroit trouué la mer." —Vimont, *Relation*, 1640, p. 36.

[6] That such was the fact, and that he did not reach the Wis-

turned his course to the southward. And the Jesuits consoled themselves, when they heard of his short-

consin river, is deduced from the language of the *Relations*; also, from a consideration of the length of the Fox and Wisconsin rivers below the "portage," where they very nearly approach each other; and from a study of the time usually employed, at an early day, in their navigation. It has, however, been extensively published that Nicolet did reach the Wisconsin, and float down its channel to within three days of the Mississippi. Now, Nicolet, in speaking of a large river upon which he had sailed, evidently intended to convey the idea of its being connected with "ce lac" (this lake); that is, with Green bay and Lake Michigan—the two being merged into one by Vimont. Hence, he must have spoken of the Fox river. But Vimont (*Relation*, 1640, p. 36) understood him as saying, "that, had he sailed three days more on a great river which *flows from* that lake, he would have found the sea."

The *Relation*, it will be noticed, says, "had he sailed three days more," etc. This implies a sailing already of some days. But such could not have been the case had he been upon the Wisconsin; as that river is only one hundred and eighteen miles in length, below the portage, and the time of its canoe navigation between three and four days only; whereas, upon the Fox, it was nine days; six, from its mouth to the Mascoutins, as previously shown, and three from the Mascoutins to the Wisconsin.

The first white men who passed up the Fox river above the Mascoutins, were Louis Joliet and Father James Marquette, with five French attendants, in June, 1673. "We knew," says Marquette, "that there was, three leagues from Maskoutens [Mascoutins], a river [Wisconsin] emptying into the Mississippi; we knew, too, that the point of the compass we were to hold to reach it, was the west-southwest; but the way is so cut up by marshes, and little lakes, that it is easy to go astray, especially as the river leading to it is so covered by wild oats, that you can hardly discover the channel."

That Marquette, instead of "three leagues" intended to say "thirty leagues" or "three days," it is evident to any one acquainted with the Fox river from the "portage" down; besides,

coming, with the hope that one day the western sea would be reached by one of their order.[1] "In passing, I will say," wrote one of their missionaries, in 1640, "that we have strong indications that one can descend through the second lake of the Hurons . . . into this sea."[2]

---

the mistake is afterward corrected in his narrative as well as on his map accompanying it, where the home of the Mascoutins is marked as indicated by Allouez in the *Relation* of 1670. See, also, the map of Joliet, before alluded to, as recently published by Gravier, where the same location is given. Joliet and Marquette were seven days in their journey from the Mascoutins to the Mississippi; this gave them three days upon the Fox and four upon the Wisconsin (including the delay at the portage). Canoes have descended from the portage in two days.

The *Relation* of 1670 (pp. 99, 100) says: "These people [the Mascoutins] are established in a very fine place, where we see beautiful plains and level country, as far as the eye reaches. Their river leads into a great river called Messisipi; [to which] their is a navigation of only six days."

But the question is evidently settled by the *Relation* of 1654 (p. 30), which says:

"It is only nine days' journey from this great lake [Green bay and Lake Michigan—'Lac de gens de mer'] to the sea;" where "the sea," referred to, is, beyond doubt, identical with "la mer" of Nicolet.

[1] "Or i'ay de fortes coniectures que c'est la mer [mentioned by Nicolet] qui respond au Nord de la Nouuelle Mexique, et que de cette mer, on auroit entrée vers le Iapon et vers la Chine, neant moins comme on ne sçait pas où tire ce grand lac, ou cette mer douce, ce seroit vne entreprise genereuse d'aller descouurir ces contrées. Nos Peres qui sont aux Hurons, inuités par quelques Algonquins, sont sur le point de donner iusques à ces gens de l'autre mer, dont i'ay parlé cy-dessus; peut estre que ce voyage se reseruera pour l'vn de nous qui auons quelque petite cognoissance de la langue Algonquine."—Vimont, *Relations*, 1640, p. 36.

[2] "The twenty-fourth day of June [1640], there arrived an En-

But why should Nicolet leave the Fox river and journey away from the Mascoutins to the southward? The answer is, that, at no great distance, lived the Illinois.[1] Their country extended eastward to Lake Michigan, and westward to the Mississippi, if not beyond it. This nation was of too much importance, and their homes too easy of access, for Nicolet not to have visited them.[2] Upon the beau-

---

glishman, with a servant, brought in boats by twenty Abnaquiois savages. He set out from the lake or river Quinibequi in Acadia, where the English have a settlement, in order to search for a passage through these countries to the North sea. . . . M. de Montmagny had him brought to Tadoussac, in order that he might return to England by way of France.

"He told us wonderful things of New Mexico. 'I learned,' said he, 'that one can sail to that country by means of the seas which lie to the north of it. Two years ago, I explored all the southern coast from Virginia to Quinebiqui to try whether I could not find some large river or some large lake which should bring me to tribes having knowledge of this sea, which is northward from Mexico. Not having found any such in these countries, I entered into the Saguené region, to penetrate, if I could, with the savages of the locality, as far as to the northern sea.'

"In passing, I will say that we have strong indications that one can descend through the second lake of the Hurons [Lake Michigan and Green bay] and through the country of the nations we have named [as having been visited by Nicolet] into this sea which he [the Englishman] was trying to find."—Vimont, *Relation*, 1640, p. 35.

[1] Synonyms: Ilinois, Ilinoues, Illini, Illiniweck, Tilliniwek, Ilimouek, Liniouck, Abimigek, Eriniouaj, etc.

[2] Vimont (*Relation*, 1640, p. 35) gives information derived from Nicolet, of the existence of the Illinois (Eriniouaj) as neighbors of the Winnebagoes. And the *Relation*, 1656 (p. 39), says: "The Liniouek [Illinois], their neighbors [that is, the neighbors of the Winnebagoes], number about sixty villages." Champlain locates a tribe, on his map of 1632, south of the Mascoutins, as a "na-

tiful prairies of what is now the state bearing their name, was this tribe located, with some **bands, probably** nearly as far northward **as** the southern **counties** of the present State **of** Wisconsin. It is not known in how **many** villages of these savages he smoked **the** pipe **of peace. From their homes he returned to the** Winnebagoes.

Before Nicolet left the country, on his return to the St. Lawrence, he obtained knowledge of the Sioux— those traders from the west who, it will be remembered, were represented as coming in canoes upon a sea **to the** Winnebagoes**; the** same **"sea," doubtless,** he came **so near to,** but **did not** behold—the Wisconsin and Mississippi rivers! **Although** without beards, and having only **a tuft of** hair upon their **crowns,** these Sioux **were no** longer mandarins—**no longer** from China or **Japan!** Bands **of** this **tribe had** pushed their way across the Mississippi, far **above the** mouth **of the** Wisconsin, **but made no further progress** eastward. They, like the **Winnebagoes, as** previously stated, were of the Dakota family. **Whether** any of them were seen by Nicolet is not **known;**[1] but **he,** doubtless, learned something of their real **character. There was yet one** tribe near the Winnebagoes **to be visited—the** Pottawattamies.[2] **They** were **located upon the islands at the** mouth of **Green**

---

tion where there is a quantity **of** buffaloes." **This nation was** probably the Illinois.

[1] **As** Nicolet proceeded no further to **the westward than six** days' sail up the Fox river of Green bay, of course, the "Nadvesiv" (Sioux) **and** "Assinipour" (Assiniboins) were not visited by him.

[2] Synonyms: Pottawottamies, Poutouatamis, Pouteouatamis, Pouutouatami, Poux, Poueatamis, Pouteouatamiouec, **etc.**

bay, and upon the main land to the southward, along the western shores of Lake Michigan.[1] On these Algonquins—for they were of that lineage—Nicolet, upon his return trip, made a friendly call.[2] Their homes were not on the line of his outward voyage, but to the south of it. Nicolet gave no information of them which has been preserved, except that they were neighbors of the Winnebagoes.[3]

So Nicolet, in the spring of 1635,[4] having previously made many friends in the far northwest for his countrymen upon the St. Lawrence, and for France, of nations of Indians, only a few of which had before been heard of, and none ever before visited by a white man; having been the first to discover Lake Michigan and "the territory northwest

---

[1] Such, at least, was their location a few years after the visit of Nicolet. The islands occupied were those farthest south.

[2] Vimont, *Relation*, 1640, p. 35. In the *Relation* of 1643, it is expressly stated that Nicolet visited some of the tribes on his return voyage.

[3] Says Margry (*Journal Général de l'Instruction Publique*, 1862): "Les peuples que le pére dit avoir été pour la plupart visités par Nicolet sont les Malhominis ou Gens de la Folle Avoine [*Menomonees*], les Ouinipigous ou Puans [*Winnebagoes*], puis les Pouteouatami [*Pottawattamies*], les Eriniouaj (ou Illinois)," etc.

[4] It is highly probable that Nicolet commenced his return trip so soon, in the spring of 1635, as the warm weather had freed Green bay of its coat of ice. Leaving the Winnebagoes, as soon as navigation opened in the spring, he would have only about ten weeks to reach the St. Lawrence by the middle of July—the time, probably, of his return, as previously mentioned; whereas, having left Quebec July 2, for the west, he had about five months before navigation closed on the lakes, to arrive out. Sault Sainte Marie must, of necessity, therefore, have been visited in *going to* the Winnebagoes.

NICOLET DISCOVERS THE NORTHWEST. 73

of the river Ohio;" having boldly struck into the wilderness for hundreds of leagues beyond the Huron villages—then the **Ultima Thule** of civilized discoveries; returned, with his seven dusky companions, by way of Mackinaw and along the south shores of the Great Manitoulin island to the home thereon of a band of Ottawas.[1] He proceeded thence to the Hurons; re-

---

[1] "To the south of the Nation of the **Beaver is** an island, in that fresh-water sea [Lake Huron], about **thirty** leagues in length, inhabited by the Outaouan [Ottawas]. These are a people come from the nation of the Standing Hair [Cheveux Relevés]."—Vimont, *Relation*, 1640, p. **34**. In William R. Smith's translation of so **much of** this *Relation* **as names** the various tribes visited **by Nicolet** (Hist. Wis., Vol. III., p. 10), what relates to the Cheveux **Relevés is** omitted—probably by accident. On a large island, corresponding as to locality with the Great Manitoulin, **is placed, on** Du Creux' **Map of** 1660, **the " natio surrectorum** capillorum "—**identical with the** Cheveux Relevés, just mentioned.

The Ottawas were first visited **by** Champlain. **This was in the** year 1615. They lived southwest of the Hurons. **It was he who** gave them the name Cheveux Relevés—Standing **Hair.** Sagard saw some of them subsequently, and calls **them** Andatahonats. See his " Histoire du Canada," p. 199.

Although, in the citation from the *Relation* of 1640, **just given, the** band of the Ottawas upon the Great Manitoulin **are said to have " come from the** nation of **the** Standing Hair," it does not fix the **residence of those from** whom they came as **in the valley** of the Ottawa river. On **the contrary,** Champlain, **in** his " Voyages" and Map, places **them in an opposite** direction, not far from the south end of the Nottawassaga **bay of Lake** Huron Says J.G. Shea (Wis. Hist. Soc. Coll., III., 135): **"There is no** trace in the early French writers of any opinion then entertained **that they** [the Ottawas] had ever been [resided] in the valley **of the Ottawa river.** After the fall **of** the Hurons [who were cut off by the Iroquois **a** number **of years** subsequent to Nicolet's visit],

7

tracing, afterward, his steps to the mouth of French river, up that stream to Lake Nipissing, and down the Mattawan and Ottawa to the St. Lawrence; journeying, upon his return, it is thought, with the savages upon their annual trading-voyage to the French settlements.[1] And Nicolet's exploration was ended.[2]

when trade was re-opened with the west, all tribes there were called Ottawas, and the river, as leading to the Ottawa country, got the name."

[1] As the traffic with the Hurons took place at Three Rivers, between the 15th and 23d of July, 1635, it is highly probable that Nicolet reached there some time during that month, on his way to Quebec.

[2] Vimont (*Relation*, 1643, p. 4) thus briefly disposes of Nicolet's return trip from the Winnebagoes: "La paix fut concluë; il retourna aux Hurons, et de la à quelque temps aux Trois Riuieres."

CHAPTER IV.

NICOLET'S SUBSEQUENT CAREER AND DEATH.

It is not difficult to imagine the interest which must have been awakened in the breast of Champlain upon the return of Nicolet to Quebec. With what delight he must have heard his recital of the particulars of the voyage! How he must have been enraptured at the descriptions of lakes of unknown extent; of great rivers never before heard of—never before seen by a Frenchman! How his imagination must have kindled when told of the numerous Indian nations which had been visited! But, above all, how fondly he hoped one day to bring all these distant countries under the dominion of his own beloved France! But the heart thus beating quick with pleasurable emotions at the prospects of future glory and renown, soon ceased its throbs. On Christmas day, 1635, Champlain died. In a chamber of the fort in Quebec, "breathless and cold, lay the hardy frame which war, the wilderness, and the sea had buffeted so long in vain."

The successor of Champlain was Marc Antoine de Bras-de-fer de Chasteaufort. He was succeeded by Charles Huault de Montmagny, who reached New France in 1636. With him came a considerable reinforcement; "and, among the rest, several men of birth and substance, with their families and dependents."

But Montmagny found the affairs of his colony in a woful condition. The "Company of One Hundred" had passed its affairs into the hands of those who were wholly engrossed in the profits of trade. Instead of sending out colonists, the Hundred Associates "granted lands, with the condition that the grantees should furnish a certain number of settlers to clear and till them, and these were to be credited to the company." The Iroquois, who, from their intercourse with the Dutch and English traders, had been supplied with firearms, and were fast becoming proficient in their use, attacked the Algonquins and Hurons—allies of the French, interrupting their canoes, laden with furs, as they descended the St. Lawrence, killing their owners, or hurrying them as captives into the forests, to suffer the horrors of torture.

At a point to which was given the name of Sillery, four miles above Quebec, a new Algonquin mission was started; still, in the immediate neighborhood of the town, the dark forests almost unbroken frowned as gloomily as when, thirty years before, Champlain founded the future city. Probably, in all New France, the population, in 1640, did not much exceed two hundred, including women and children. On the eighteenth of May, 1642, Montreal began its existence. The tents of the founders were "inclosed with a strong palisade, and their altar covered by a provisional chapel, built, in the Huron mode, of bark." But the Iroquois had long before become the enemies of the French, sometimes seriously threatening Quebec. So, upon the Island of Montreal, every precaution was taken to avoid surprise. Solid structures of wood soon defied the attacks of the savages;

and, to give greater security to the colonists, Montmagny caused a fort to be erected at the mouth of the Richelieu, in the following August. But the end of the year 1642 brought no relief to the Algonquins or Hurons, and little to the French, from the ferocious Iroquois.

It was not long after Nicolet's return to Quebec, from his visit to " the People of the Sea," and neighboring nations, before he was assigned to Three Rivers by Champlain, where he was to continue his office of commissary and interpreter; for, on the ninth of December, 1635, he " came to give advice to the missionaries who were dwelling at the mission that a young Algonquin was sick; and that it would be proper to visit him."[1] And, again, on the seventh of the following month, he is found visiting, with one of the missionaries, a sick Indian, near the fort, at Three Rivers.[2] His official labors were performed to the great satisfaction of both French and Indians,

---

[1] " Le neufiesme de Decembre, iustement le lendemain de la feste de la Conception, le sieur Iean Nicolet, Truchement pour les Algonquins aux Trois Riuieres, vint donner aduis aux Peres, qui de meuroient en la Residence de la Conception sise au mesme lieu, qu'vn ieune Algonquin se trounoit mal, et qu'il seroit à prospos de le visiter."—Le Jeune, *Relation*, 1636, p. 8.

[2] " Le septiesme de Ianuier de cette année mil six cens trente six, le fils d'vn grand Sorcier ou Iongleur fut faict Chrestien, son pere s'y accordant apres de grandes resistances qu'il en fit: car, comme nos Peres éuentoient ses mines, et la decreditoient, il ne pouuoit les supporter en sa Cabane. Cependant comme son fils tiroit à la mort, ils prierent le sieur Nicolet de faire son possible pour sauuer cette âme : ils s'en vont donc le Pere Quentin et luy en cette maison d'écorce, pressent fortement ce Sauuage de consentir au baptesme de son petit fils."—Le Jeune, *Relation*, 1636, p. 10.

by whom he was equally and sincerely loved. He was constantly assisting the missionaries, so far as his time would permit, in the conversion of the savages, whom he knew how to manage and direct as he desired, and with a skill that could hardly find its equal. His kindness won their esteem and respect. His charity seemed, indeed, to know no bounds.[1] As interpreter for one of the missionaries, he accompanied him from Three Rivers on a journey some leagues distant, on the twelfth of April, 1636, to visit

---

[1] " Le trente-vniesme [of December, 1635], vne fille agée d'enuiron seize ans fut baptisée, et nommée Anne par vn de nos François. Le Pere Buteux l'instruisant luy dit, que si estant Chrestienne elle venoit à mourir, son âme iroit au Ciel dans les ioyes eternelles. A ce mot de mourir, elle eut vne si grande frayeur, qu'elle ne voulut plus iamais prester l'oreille au Pere; on luy enuoya le Sieur Nicolet truchement, qui exerce volontiers semblables actions de charité; elle l'escoute paisiblement; mais comme ses occupations le diuertissent ailleurs, il ne la pouuoit visiter si souuent : c'est pourquoy le Pere Quentin s'efforça d'apprendre les premiers rudimens du Christianisme en Sauuage, afin de la pouur instruire. Cela luy reüssit si bien, que cette pauure fille ayant pris goust à cette doctrine salutaire, desira le Baptesme que la Pere luy accorda. La grace a plusieurs effects : on remarqua que cette fille, fort dedaigneuse et altiere de son naturel, deuint fort douce et traittable, estant Chrestienne.—Ibid.

" Il [Nicolet] . . . continua sa charge de Commis et Interprete [at Three Rivers] auec vne satisfaction grande des François et des Sauuages, desquels il estoit esgalement et vniquement aymé. Il conspiroit puissamment, autant que sa charge le permettoit, auec nos Peres, pour la conuersion de ces peuples, lesquels il sçauoit manier et tourner où il vouloit d'vne dexterité qui à peine trouuera son pareil."—Vimont, *Relation*, 1643, p. 4.

Compare, also, *Relation*, 1637, p. 24.

some savages who were sick; thus constantly administering to their sufferings.¹

Notwithstanding the colonists of New France were living in a state of temporal and spiritual vassalage, yet the daring Nicolet, and others of the interpreters of Champlain, although devout Catholics and friendly to the establishment of missions among the Indian nations, were not Jesuits, nor in the service of these fathers; neither was their's the mission work, in any sense, which was so zealously prosecuted by these disciples of Loyola.* They were a small class of men, whose home—some of them—was the forest, and their companions savages. They followed the Indians in their roamings, lived with them, grew familiar with their language, allied themselves, in some cases, with their women, and often became oracles in the camp and leaders on the war-path. Doubtless, when they returned from their rovings, they often had pressing need of penance and absolution. Several of them were men of great intelligence and an invincible courage. From hatred of restraint, and love of wild and adventurous independence, they encountered privations and dangers scarcely less than those to which the Jesuit exposed himself from motives widely

---

¹ "Le deuxiéme iouer d'Auril, le Pere Quentin fit vn voyage à quelques lieuës des Trois Riuieres [Three Rivers], pour quelques malades, dont on nous auoit donné aduis. Le fruict qu'il en rapporta fut d'auoir exposé plusieurs fois sa vie pour Dieu, parmy les dangers des glaces et du mauuais temps. Il se contenta de leur donner quelque instruction, sans en baptiser aucun, ne les voyant ny en peril de mort, ny suffisamment instruits. Le sieur Iean Nicolet luy seruit de truchement, auec sa charité et fidelité ordinaire, dont nos Peres tirent de grands seruices en semblables occasions."—Le Jeune, *Relation*, 1636, pp. 57, 58.

different :—he, from religious zeal, charity, and the hope of paradise; they, simply because they liked it. Some of the best families of Canada claim descent from this vigorous and hardy stock.[1]

"The Jesuits from the first had cherished the plan of a seminary for Huron boys at Quebec. The governor and the company favored the design; since not only would it be an efficient means of spreading the faith and attaching the tribe to the French interest, but the children would be pledges for the good behavior of the parents, and hostages for the safety of missionaries and traders in the Indian towns. In the summer of 1636, Father Daniel, descending from the Huron country, worn, emaciated, his cassock patched and tattered, and his shirt in rags, brought with him a boy, to whom two others were soon added; and through the influence of the interpreter, Nicolet, the number was afterward increased by several more. One of them ran away, two ate themselves to death, a fourth was carried home by his father, while three of those remaining stole a canoe, loaded it with all they could lay their hands upon, and escaped in triumph with their plunder."[2]

Nicolet frequently visited Quebec. Upon one of

---

[1] Adapted from Parkman's "Jesuits in North America," pp. 165, 166.

[2] Parkman's "Jesuits in North America," pp. 167, 168, citing the *Relations* of 1637 and 1638. Father Le Jeune (*Relation*, 1636, p. 75) says: "Comme i'écry cecy le vingt-huictiéme d'Aoust, voila que le Pere Buteux me mande le départ du Pere Ioques, l'arriuée d'vne autre troupe de Hurons, de qui le sieur Nicolet a encore obtenu trois icunes garçons, sur le rapport que leur ont fait leurs compagnons du bon traittement que Monsieur le General et tous les autres François leur auoient fait."

these occasions he had a narrow escape. He found the St. Lawrence incumbered with ice. Behind him there came so great a quantity of it that he was compelled to get out of his canoe and jump upon one of the floating pieces. He saved himself with much difficulty and labor. This happened in April, 1637.[1] On the twenty-seventh of the same month Nicolet was present at Quebec, on the occasion of a deputation of Indians from Three Rivers waiting upon the governor, asking a favor at his hands promised by Champlain. He was consulted as to what the promise of the former governor was.[2]

In June, he was sent, it seems, up from the fort at Three Rivers to ascertain whether the Iroquois were approaching. He went as far as the river Des Prairies —the name for the Ottawa on the north side of the island of Montreal.[3] In August, the enemy threatened Three Rivers in force. The French and Indians in the fort could not be decoyed into danger. However, a boat was sent up the St. Lawrence, conducted by Nicolet. The bark approached the place where the Iroquois were, but could not get within gun-shot; yet a random discharge did some execution. The enemy were judged to be about five hundred strong. Although the fort at Three Rivers was thus seriously threatened, no attack was made.[4]

On the seventh of October, 1637, Nicolet was married at Quebec to Marguerite Couillard, a god-child of

---
[1] Le Jeune, *Relation*, 1637, p. 78.
[2] Ib., p. 81.
[3] Ib., p. 84.
[4] Ib., p. 89.

Champlain.¹ The fruit of this marriage was but one child—a daughter. Nicolet continued his residence at Three Rivers, largely employed in his official duties of commissary and interpreter, remaining there until the time of his death.² In 1641, he, with one of the Jesuit fathers, was very busy in dealing with a large force of Iroquois that was threatening the place.³

About the first of October, 1642, Nicolet was called down to Quebec from Three Rivers, to take the place of his brother-in-law, M. Olivier le Tardiff, who was General Commissary of the Hundred Partners, and who sailed on the seventh of that month for France. The change was a very agreeable one to Nicolet, but he did not long enjoy it; for, in less than a month after his arrival, in endeavoring to make a trip to his

---

¹ See Ferland's "Cours D' Histoire du Canada," Vol. I., p. 326; also, his "Notes sur les Resigistres de Notre-Dame de Québec," p. 30, notes; and Gravier's "Découvertes et Établissements de Cavalier de la Salle," p. 47.

Nicolet's wife was a daughter of Guillaume Couillard and Guillemette Hébert. Nicolet's marriage contract was dated at Quebec, October 22, 1637, several days subsequent to his nuptials. This was not an uncommon thing in New France in early days, but has not been allowed in Canada for about a century past. The contract was drawn up by Guitet, a notary of Quebec. There were present François Derré de Gand, Commissaire-Général; Olivier le Tardif; Noël Juchereau; Pierre De la Porte; Guillaume Huboust; Guillaume Hébert; Marie Rollet aïeule de la future épouse; Claude Racine; Etienne Racine.

² The presence of Nicolet at Three Rivers during all these years (except from March 19, 1638, to January 9, 1639) is shown by reference to the *Relations*, and to the church register of that place. See Appendix, I., as to the latter.

³ Vimont, *Relation*, 1641, p. 41.

place of residence to release an Indian prisoner in the possession of a band of Algonquins, who were slowly torturing him, his zeal and humanity cost him his life.¹ On the 27th of October,² he embarked at Quebec, near seven o'clock in the evening, in the launch of M. de Savigny, which was headed for Three Rivers. He had not yet reached Sillery, when a northeast squall raised a terrible tempest on the St. Lawrence and filled the boat. Those who were in it did not immediately go down; they clung some time to the launch. Nicolet had time to say to M. de Savigny, "Save yourself, sir; you can swim; I can not. I am going to God. I recommend to you my wife and daughter." ³

---

¹ Monsieur Oliuier, Commis General de Messieurs de la Compagnie, estant venu l'an passé en France, le dit sieur Nicollet descendit à Quebec en sa place, auec vne ioye, et consolation sensible qu'il eut de se voir dans la paix et la deuotion de Quebec. Mais il n'en ioüit pas long-temps: car vn mois ou deux aprés son arriuée, faisant vn voyage aux Trois Riuieres pour la deliurance d'vn prisonnier Sauuage, son zele luy cousta la vie, qu'il perdit dans le naufrage."—Vimont, *Relation*, 1643, p. 4.

² I'adiousteray icy vn mot de la vie et de la mort de Monsieur Nicollet, Interprete et Commis de Messieurs de la Compagnie de la Nouuelle France; il mourut dix iours apres le Pere [Charles Raymbault, décédé le 22 Octobre, 1642], il auoit demeuré vingt-cinq ans en ces quartiers."—Vimont, *Relation*, 1643, p. 3. The incorrectness of this date as to the death of Nicolet will hereafter be shown.

³ "Il [*Nicolet*] sembarqua à Quebec sur les sept heures du soir, dans la chalouppe de Monsieur de Sauigny, qui tiroit vers les Trois Riuieres, ils n'estoient pas encor arriuez à Sillery, qu'vn coup de vent de Nord Est, qui auoit excité vne horrible tempeste sur la grande riuiere, remplit la chalouppe d'eau et la coula à fond, apres luy auoir fait faire deux ou trois tours dans

The wild waves tore the men, one after another, from the boat, which had capsized and floated against a rock, and four, including Nicolet, sank to rise no more.[1] M. de Savigny alone cast himself into the

---

l'eau. Ceux qui estoient dedans n'allerent pas incontinent à fond, ils s'attacherent quelque temps à la challouppe. Monsieur Nicollet eut loisir de dire à Monsieur de Sauigny: Monsieur, sauuez-vous, vous sçauez nager; ie ne le sçay pas. Pour moy ie m'en vay à Dieu; ie vous recommande ma femme et ma fille."— Vimont, *Relation*, 1643, p. 4.

Nicolet's daughter afterwards married Jean-Baptiste le Gardeur de Repentigny, entering into a family which was one of the most considerable in French America. Her son, Augustin le Gardeur de Courtemanche,—"officier dans les troupes, se distingua, par de longs et utiles services dans l'ouest, fut un digne contemporain de Nicolas Perot, de même qu'un honorable rejeton de sou grandpère Nicolet."—Sulte's "Mélanges D'Histoire et de Littérature," p. 446.

[1] It is reasonably certain that the day of Nicolet's death was October 27, 1642. Compare Margry, in *Journal Général de l'Instruction Publique*, 1862. A recent writer says:

"Le 29 septembre 1642, aux Trois-Rivières, le Père Jean de Brebeuf baptista deux petites filles de race algonquine dont les parrains et marraines furent 'Jean Nicolet avec Perrette (nom indien), et Nicolas Marsolet (l'interprète), avec Marguerite Couillard, femme de M. Nicolet.'

"Le 7 octobre suivant eut lieu, à Québec, le départ des navires pour la France. (*Relation*, 1643, p. 46.) Cette Relation écrite vers la fin de l'été de 1643, raconte ce qui s'est passé après le départ des navires de 1642.

"Le sieur Olivier le Tardif partit pour la France cet automne, 1642, et fut remplacé à Québec, dans sa charge de commis-général de la compagnie des Cent-Associés, par son beau-frère Nicolet, qui descendit des Trois-Rivières expressément pour cela (*Relation*, 1643, p. 4), par conséquent entre le 29 septembre et le 7 octobre.

"Le 19 octobre, un sauvage d'une nation alliée aux Iroquois

water, and swam among the waves, which were like
small mountains. The launch was not very far from
the shore, but it was pitch dark, and the bitter cold
had covered the river banks with ice. Savigny, feeling his resolution and his strength failing him, made

---

fut amené captif aux Trois-Rivières par les Algonquins de ce
lieu, qui le condamnèrent à périr sur le bûcher. (*Relation*, 1643,
p. 46.) Les Pères Jésuites et M. des Rochers, le commandant du
fort, ayant épuisé tous les arguments qu'ils croyaient pouvoir employer pour induire ces barbares à ne pas faire mourir leur prisonnier, envoyèrent un messager à Québec avertir Nicolet de ce
qui se passait et réclamer son assistance. (*Relation*, 1643, p. 4.)
"Ces pourparlers et ces démarches paraissent avoir occupé
plusieurs jours.

"A cette nouvelle, Nicolet, n'écoutant que son cœur, s'embarqua à Québec, dans la chaloupe de M. Chavigny, vers les sept
heures du soir. L'embarcation n'était pas arrivée à Sillery, qu'un
coup de vent du nord-est qui avait soulevé une grosse tempête, la
remplit d'eau et la coula à fond. M. de Chavigny seul se sauva.
La nuit était très-noire et il faisait un froid âpre qui avait couvert
de 'bordages' les rives du fleuve. (*Relation*, 1643, p. 4.)

"Dans ses *Notes sur les registres* de Notre-Dame de Québec, M.
l'abbé Ferland nous donne le texte de l'acte qui suit: 'Le 29
octobre, on fit les funérailles de monsieur Nicollet et de trois
hommes de M. de Chavigny, noyés dans une chaloupe qui allait
de Québec à Sillery ; les corps ne furent point trouvés.'

"M. de Chavigny demeurait à Sillery. Il est probable que
Nicolet comptait repartir de là le lendemain, soit à la voile (en
chaloupe) ou en canot d'écorce, selon l'état du fleuve, pour atteindre les Trois-Rivières.

"Le captif des Algonquins ayant été délivré par l'entremise de
M. des Rochers, arriva à Québec douze jours après le naufrage de
Nicolet (*Relation*, 1643, p. 4), le 9 novembre (*Relation*, 1643, p. 44),
ce qui fixerait au 27 ou 28 octobre la date demandée.

"Comme ce malheur eut lieu à la nuit close, pendant une tempête, il est raisonable de supposer que la recherche des cadavres
ne put se faire que le lendemain, surtout lorsque nous songeons
que Sillery n'est pas Québec, quoiqu'assez rapproché. Le service

a vow to God, and a little after, reaching down with his feet, he felt the bottom, and stepping out of the water, he reached Sillery half dead. For quite a while he was unable to speak; then, at last, he recounted the fatal accident which, besides the death of Nicolet—disastrous to the whole country—had cost him three of his best men and a large part of his property. He and his wife suffered this great loss, in a barbarous country, with great patience and resignation to the will of God, and without losing any of their courage.[1]

---

funebrè dût être célébré le troisième jour, et non pas le lendemain de l'événement en question.

"J'adopte donc la date du lundi 27 octobre comme celle de la mort de Nicolet.

"Il est vrai que la *Relation* citée plus haut nous dit (p. 3) que le Père Charles Raymbault décéda le 22 octobre, et que la mort de Nicolet eut lieu dix jours après; mais l'acte du 29 octobre au registre de Québec renverse ce calcul de dix jours qui nous mènerait au 1er ou 2 novembre.

"La même *Relation* (p. 4) dit aussi que Nicolet périt un mois ou deux après son arrivée à Québec, tandis que nous voyons par ce que j'expose ci-dessus qu'il n'a guère été plus de trois semaines absent des Trois-Rivières avant de partir pour sa fatale expédition.

"La date du 27 octobre paraît irréfutable."—M. Sulte, in *L'Opinion Publique*, Montreal, July 24, 1879.

[1] Les vagues les arracherent tous les vns aprés les autres de la chalouppe, qui flottoit renuersée contre vne roche. Monsieur de Sauigny seul se ietta à l'eau et nagea parmy des flots et des vagues qui resembloient à de petites montagnes. La Chalouppe n'estoit pas bien loin du riuage; mais il estoit nuict toute noire, et faisoit vn froid aspre, qui auoit desia glacé les bords de la riuiere. Le dit sieur de Sauigny, sentant le cœur et les forces qui luy manquoient, fit vn vœu à Dieu, et peu aprés frappant du pied il sent la terre, et se tirant hors de l'eau,

NICOLET'S SUBSEQUENT CAREER AND DEATH. 87

The savages of Sillery, at the report of Nicolet's shipwreck, ran to the place, and not seeing him any where, displayed indescribable sorrow. It was not the first time he had exposed himself to danger of death for the good of the Indians. He had done so frequently. Thus perished John Nicolet, in the waters of the great river of Canada—the red man and the Frenchman alike mourning his untimely fate.[1]

Twelve days after the shipwreck, the prisoner to the Algonquins, for whose deliverance Nicolet started on his journey, arrived at Sillery—the commander at Three Rivers, following the order of the governor, having ransomed him. He was conducted to the hospital of the place to be healed of the injuries he had received from his captors. They had stripped the flesh from his arms, in some places to the bone. The nuns at the hospital cared for him with much sympathy, and cured him so quickly that in a month's

---

s'en vint en nostre maison à Sillery à demy mort. Il demeura assez long-temps sans pouuoir parler; puis enfin il nous raconta le funeste accident, qui outre la mort de Monsieur Nicollet, dommageable à tout le pays, luy auoit perdue trois de ses meilleurs hommes et vne grande partie de son meuble et de ses prouisions. Luy et Mademoiselle sa femme ont porté cette perte signallée dans vn pays barbare, auec vne grande patience et resignation à la volonté de Dieu, et sans rien diminuer de leur courage.—Vimont, *Relation*, 1643, p. 4.

[1] "Les Sauuages de Sillery, au bruit du nauffrage de Monsieur Nicollet, courent sur le lieu, et ne le voyant plus paroistre, en tesmoignent des regrets indicibles. Ce n'estoit pas la premiere fois que cet homme s'estoit exposé ou danger de la mort pour le bien et le salut des Sauuages: il l'a faict fort souuent, et nous à laissé des exemples qui sont au dessus de l'estat d'vn homme marié, et tiennent de le vie Apostolique et laissent vne enuie au plus feruent Religieux de l'imiter."—Vimont, *Relation*, 1643, p. 4.

time he was able to return to his country. All the neophytes showed him as much compassion and charity as the Algonquins had displayed of cruelty. They gave him two good, Christianized savages to escort him as far as the country of a neighboring tribe of his own, to the end that he might reach his home in safety.[1]

After the return of the French to Quebec, the Jesuits, as previously mentioned, were commissioned with the administration of spiritual affairs in New France. Some of these turned their attention to the Europeans; the rest were employed in missions among the savages. In the autumn of 1635, the residences and missions of Canada contained fifteen Fathers and five Brothers of the Society of Jesus. At Quebec, there were also formed two seculars—ecclesiastics. One of these was a brother of Nicolet.[2] He had come

---

[1] "Douze iours aprés leur naufrage, le prisonnier pour la deliurance duquel il [Nicolet] s'estoit embarqué, arriua icy. Monsieur des Roches commandant aux Trois Riuieres, suiuant l'ordre de Monsieur le Gouuerneur, l'auoit racheté. Il mit pied à terre à Sillery, et de là fut conduit à l'Hospital pour estre pansé des playes et blessures que les Algonquins luy auoient faites apres sa capture: ils luy auoient emporté la chair des bras, en quelques endroits iusques aux os. Les Religieuses hospitalieres le receurent auec beaucoup de charité, et le firent panser fort soigneusement, en sorte qu'en trois semaines ou vn mois, il fut en estat de retourner en son pays. Tous nos Neophytes luy tesmoignerent autant de compassion et de charité que les Algonquins de là haut luy auoient montré de cruauté: ils luy donnerent deux bons Sauuages Christiens, pour le conduire iusques aux pays des Abnaquiois, qui sont voisins de sa nation."—Vimont, *Relation*, 1643, pp. 4, 5.

[2] His name was Gilles Nicolet. He was born in Cherbourg, and came to Canada in 1635. He is one of the first "prêtres seculiers"—that is, not belonging to congregations or institutes, such

from Cherbourg to join him upon the St. Lawrence; and, during his residence in the colony, which was continued to 1647, he was employed in visiting French settlements at a distance from Quebec.[1] Another brother—Pierre—who was a navigator, also resided in Canada, but left the country some time after Nicolet's death.[2] The widow of Nicolet was married at Quebec, in 1646, to Nicholas Macard.

Nicolet's discoveries, although not immediately followed up because of the hostility of the Iroquois and the lack of the spirit of adventure in Champlain's successor, caused, finally, great results. He had unlocked the door to the Far West, where, afterward, were seen the fur-trader, the *voyageur*, the Jesuit missionary, and the government agent. New France was extended to the Mississippi and beyond; yet Nicolet did not live to witness the progress of French trade and conquest in the countries he had discovered.

The name of the family of Nicolet appears to have been extinguished in Canada, with the departure of M. Gilles Nicolet, priest, already mentioned; but the respect which the worthy interpreter had deserved induced the people of Three Rivers to perpetuate his memory. The example had been given before his death. We read in the *Relation* of 1637 that the river St. John, near Montreal (now the river Jésus), took its

---

as the Jesuits and the Récollets—whose name appears on the Quebec parochial register.

[1] Those of the coast of Beaupre, between Beauport and Cape Tourmente. Ferland's "Cours D'Histoire du Canada," Vol. I., pp. 276, 277.

[2] Sulte's "Mélanges D'Histoire et de Littérature," p. 446.

8

name from *John* Nicolet. To-day Canada has the river, the lake, the falls, the village, the city, the college, and the county of Nicolet.[1] From the United States—especially from the Northwest—equal honor is due.

"History can not refrain from saluting Nicolet as a disinterested traveler, who, by his explorations in the interior of America, has given clear proofs of his energetic character, and whose merits have not been disputed, although subsequently they were temporarily forgotten." The first fruits of his daring were gathered by the Jesuit fathers even before his death; for, in the autumn of 1641, those of them who were among the Hurons received a deputation of Indians occupying "the country around a rapid, in the midst of the channel by which Lake Superior empties into Lake Huron," inviting them to visit their tribe.

---

[1] Benjamin Sulte, in *l'Opinion Publique*, 1873. The writer adds:
"La rivière Nicolet est formée de deux rivières qui gardent chacune ce nom; l'une au nord est sort d'un lac appelé Nicolet, dans le comté de Wolfe, township de Ham; l'autre, celle du sud ouest, qui passe dans le comté de Richmond, a donné le nom de Nicolet à un village situé sur ses bords, dans le township de Shipton. Ce village que les Anglais nomment 'Nicolet Falls' est un centre d'industrie prospère. La ville de Nicolet, ainsi que le collége de ce nom, sont situés près de la décharge des eaux réunies de ces deux rivières au lac Saint-Pierre.

"Peu d'années après la mort de Jean Nicolet, les trifluviens donnaient déjà son nom à la rivière en question, malgré les soins que prenaient les fonctionnaires civils de ne désigner cet endroit que par les mots 'la rivière de Laubia ou la rivière Cressé.' M. de Laubia ne concède la seigneurie qu'en 1672, et M. Cressé ne l'obtint que plus tard, mais avant ces deux seigneurs, la rivière portrait le nom de Nicolet, et l'usage en prevalut en dépit des tentatives faites pour lui imposer d'autres dénominations."

These " missionaries were not displeased with the opportunity thus presented of knowing the countries lying beyond Lake Huron, which no one of them had yet traversed ;" so Isaac Jogues and Charles Raymbault were detached to accompany the Chippewa deputies, and view the field simply, not to establish a mission. They passed along the shore of Lake Huron, northward, and pushed as far up St. Mary's strait as the "Sault," which they reached after seventeen days' sail from their place of starting. There they—the first white men to visit the Northwest after Nicolet—harangued two thousand of that nation, and other Algonquins. Upon their return to the St. Lawrence, Jogues was captured by the Iroquois, and Raymbault died on the twenty-second of October, 1642—a few days before the death of Nicolet.

APPENDIX.

I.—EXTRACTS (LITERAL) FROM THE **PARISH** CHURCH REGISTER, OF **THREE** RIVERS, CANADA, CONCERNING NICOLET.

I.

"Le 27 du mois de décembre 1635, fut baptisée par le Père Jacques Buteux [1] une petite fille âgée d'environ deux ans, fille du capitaine des Montagnetz Capitainal.[2] Elle fut nommée *Marie* par M. de Maupertuis et M. Nicollet ses parrains. Elle s'appelait en sauvage 8minag8m8c8c8." [3]

II.

"Le 30 du mois de Mai 1636, une jeune Sauvagesse Algonquine instruite par le Père Jacques Buteux, fut baptisée par le Père Claude Quentin et nommée Françoise par M. Nicollet son parrain." [1637, 7th

---

[1] Father Buteux resided in Three Rivers from the year of the establishment of that place, 1634, to 1651 when, on his second trip to the upper St. Maurice he was killed by the Iroquois.

[2] Capitanal, chief of the Montagnais Indians, is the **man who** did the most amongst his people to impress upon **the** mind **of** Champlain the necessity of erecting a fort at 3-Rivers. He died **in** 1635. See *Relation*, 1633, p. 26; 1635, p. 21.

[3] The figure "8" in such words is, as before mentioned, supposed to be equivalent to "w," "**we,**" or "**oo,**" in English. Ante, p. 46, **note.**

October. At Quebec. Marriage of Nicolet with Marguerite Couillard.]

III.

"Le 18 novembre 1637 fut baptisée (par le Père Claude Pijart) une femme Algonquine. Elle fut nommée Marie par Nicollet son parrain. Elle est décédée."

IV.

"Le 18 décembre 1637 fut baptisé par le Père Jacques Buteux un petit Alonquin âgé d'environ deux ans, et fut nommé Jean par M. Nicollet. Il est décédé."

V.

"1638. Le 19 de mars, jour de Saint-Joseph, fut baptisé par le Père Jacques Buteux, dans notre chapelle avec les cérémonies de l'Eglise, Anisk8ask8si, et fut nommé Paul par M. Nicollet, son parrain ; sa marraine fut mademoiselle Marie Le Neuf.[1] Il est décéde." [The Parish Register for 1638 stops at the date of 24th May, the remainder being lost.]

VI.

"Le 9 janvier 1639, le Père Jacques Delaplace baptisa solennellement, en notre chapelle, une petite fille âgée de 2 ans appelée Nitig8m8sta8an, fille de Papitchitikpabe8, capitaine de la Petite-Nation. Elle

---

[1] Le Neuf. Name of a large family, belonging to the nobility. Jean Godefroy having married Marie Le Neuf, they all came together (36 people) to Canada, when the branch of Le Gardeur settled at Quebec and that of Le Neuf proper at 3-Rivers. Throughout the history of Canada, we met with members of that group.

APPENDIX. 95

fut nommée Louise par M. Nicolet. Sa marraine fut une Sauvagesse baptisée, **femme de feu Thebachit.**"

VII.

" Le 4 mars 1639, le Révérend Père Jacques Buteux baptisa solennellement en notre chappelle les deux **enfants de 8ab8sch8stig8an**, Algonquin de l'Isle, et **Sk8esens, sa femme.** Le fils âgé d'environ quatre ans fut nommé Thomas par M. Nicolet, et Alizon,[1] et la fille âgée d'environ six ans, fut nommée Marguerite par M. de Malapart [2] et **Madame Nicolet.**".

VIII.

" 1639. Le huitième Mars, le R. P. Buteux **baptiza** solennellement Nipiste8ignan âgé d'environ vingt ans, fils **de François Nenascouat,**[3] habitant de Sillery. François **Marguerie et Madame Nicolet le** nommèrent **Vincent.**"

IX.

" Le 20 mars 1639 le R. P. Buteux **baptiza** solennellement en notre chapelle **Louis Godefroy,** fils de M. Jean Godefroy [4] **et de** Damoisselle Marie Le Neuf.

[1] Alizon is **the** family name of the wife of Gourdin, **the brewer,** who resided at the Fort of Three-Rivers as early as **1634.**

[2] Malapart **was at that time acting as** governor of the post.

[3] Nenascoumat, **an Indian chief, is much** connected with **the** history of the first settlement **of his people at** 3-Rivers **and Sillery,** from 1634 to about 1650.

[4] Jean Godefroy, the principal man **who caused** French **people to come direct** from France to settle at **Three-Rivers,** as early as **1636. He had** been in Canada for many years before. His brother Thomas is well known in the history of those years for his **services** both to **the** missionaries and to the colonists; he was

Son parrain fut Thomas Godefroy, et sa marraine Madame Marguerite Nicolet."

X.

"Anno Domini 1639 die 16 Julii, Ego Claudius Pijart vices agens parochi ecclesiæ B. V. Conceptæ ad Tria Flumina baptizavit cum ceremoniis, Ognatem, 4 circiter menses, natem patre 8kar8st8, *de la Petite-Nation*, et matre 8sasamit8n8k8e8. Partrinus fuit D. Jaunes Nicolets Interp."

XI.

"1639. Anno Domini 1639, di 20 julii Ego Claudius Pijart vices agens parochi ecclesiæ Beatæ Virginis Conceptæ ad Tria Flumina baptizavit cum ceremoniis Marinum, filium patria insularibus; patrinus idem qui supra Joannes Nicolet. Infant natus 2 menses. Il est décédé."

XII.

"Anno Domini 1639, die 30. Julii, Ego Jacobus Buteux vices agens parochi ecclesiæ B. V. C. at Tria Flumina, baptizavit Algonquiuensen natum 40 circiter annos nomine Abdom Chibanagouch, patria insularem, quem nominavit Dominus Joannes Nicolet nunc Joseph 8masatick8e." [1639. 9th October. Nicolet was present at the wedding of Jean Joliet and Marie d'Abancour, at Quebec. Louis Joliet, son of the above, was the discoverer of the Upper Mississippi.]

---

burned by the Iroquois. Louis, son of Jean, became King's Attorney. Jean was raised to the rank of nobleman by Louis XIV. His descendants are still in the district of 3-Rivers.

XIII.

"1639. Die 7 Decembris. Ego Jacobus Buteux baptizavit infentem annum circiter natum, nomine Ombrosuim Katank8quich, filium defuncti 8tagamechk8, patria 88echkarini, quedu educat N8ncheak8s mulier patria insulare, patrinus fuit Joannes Nicolet."

XIV.

"1640. Die 6 Januarii, ego Jacobus Buteux, baptizavit cum ceremoniis Mariam Ik8esens patria insularem natam circiter 28 annos, cujus patrinus fuit Joannes Nicolet et Joanna La Meslée,[1] exur pistoris. Elle est avec 8tchakin."

XV.

"Anno 1640, 4 Decemb. statim post portam mortuus sepultus in cœmeterio item filius Domini Joannis Nicolet interpretis." [In the margin is written : " Ignace Nicolet."]

XVI.

"Anno 1640. Die 14 Januarii, ego Carolus Raymbaut[2] baptizavi cum cæremoniis Franciscum missameg natum circiter 4 annos filium Ching8a defuncti, patria

---

[1] Christophe Crevier, sieur de la Mêlée, settled in 3-Rivers in 1639. Like that of Godefroy, the family became very numerous and prosperous. The descendants of Crevier still exist in the district of 3-Riv. François Crevier, born 13th May 1640 was killed by the Iroquois in Three Rivers when 13 years old only.

[2] Father Raymbault is the same that accompanied Father Jogues in the spring of the year 1642 to what is now Sault Ste. Marie, Michigan. He died, it will be remembered, in the fall of 1642. Ante, p. 91.

—— Khin8chebink educatur apud 8abirini8ich Patrinus fuit D. Franciscus de Champflour[1] moderator; matrina Margarita Couillard uxor D. Nicolet interpretis."

XVII.

"14o. die Maii 1640. Ego Carolus Raymbault baptisavi cum cæremoniis Franciscum pridie natum filium Christophori Crevier pistoris, Et Joanna Ennart conjugum Rothomagensium. Patrinus fuit Dominus Franciscum de Champflour moderator et Dna Margarita Couillard conjux interpretis (est in Galliæ)."
[On the 2d day of september, 1640 Nicolet was present at Quebec at the wedding of Nicolas Bonhomme.]

XVIII.

"Anno Domini 1640 die 25 Decembris, ipso Jesu Domini Nostri Nativitatis die ego Joannes Dequen, Societatis Jesu sacerdos vices agens Rectoris Ecclesiæ conceptionis beatæ Virginis ad Tria Flumina dicta, baptizavi solemniter in eodem ecclesia Paulum 8abirim8ich annum Trigesimum cerciter quintum doctrinæ Christianæ rudimentis sufficienter instructum. Patrinus fuit Joannes Nicolet, interpret. huic nomen Pauli impasuit; matrina fuit Maria Le Neuf."

XIX.

"Anno Domini 1641 dia 1o Aprilis. Ego Josephus Poncet, Societatis Jesu, baptizavi puellam recens natam patre Abdon 8maskik8cia, matre Michtig8k8e,

---

[1] Champflour left for France in the autumn of 1645. For several years, he had been governor of 3-Rivers.

nomen Cecilia impositum est. Patrinus fuit . . . Lavallée;[1] Matrina Margarita Couillard uxor Joannis Nicolet interpretis."

XX.

"1o Aprilis Anno 1642 Ego Josephus Poncet Societatis Jesu, in ecclesiæ immaculatæ conceptionis B. V. Mariæ, baptisavi puellum recens natam. Patre Joannes Nicolet. Matre Margarita Couillard ejus uxor. Nomen Margarita impositum. Patrinus fuit Dnus Jacobus Ertel;[2] matrina Dna Joanna Le Marchand,[3] viduæ Dni Leneuf."

XXI.

" Tertio Julii Anni 1642, ego Joannes de Brebeuf, Societatis Jesu, tunc vices agens parochi in ecclesiæ Immaculatæ Conceptionis ad Tria Flumina baptisavi infantem recens natam. Patre Dno Jacobo Hartel. Matre Marie Marguerie[4] ejus uxore. Nomine Francisco impositum. Patrinus fuit: Franciscus Marguerye, infantio avanculus; matrina Margarita Couillart domini Joannis Nicolet uxor."

---

[1] :laude Jutra lit Lavallée was one of the first settlers of 3-Rivers, where his descendants still exist.

Jacques Hertel, married to Marie Marguerie. He held land at 3-Rivers before the foundation of the Fort. Died 1652. His son François was one of the greatest sons of Canada. Louis XIV. made him a nobleman. His descendants are still in Canada. Like Godefroy, Crevier, and Le Neuf, the Hertels have held their position for 250 years.

[2] Jeanne Le Marchand, widow, was the mother of Le Neuf.

[4] François Marguerie succeeded Nicolet as Interpreter at 3-Rivers. He has left his name to a river flowing into the St. Lawrence, in the county of Nicolet opposite the town of 3-Rivers.

XXII.

"Anno Domini 1642, 29 Septembris, Ego Joannes de Brebeuf, Societatis Jesu sacerdos, baptisavi solemniter in ecclesiæ Immaculata Conceptionis ad Tria Flumina, duos puellas recens nata, unum ex patre Augustino Chipak8etch et matre 8t8ribik8e; Alizon dicta est a patrinis Joanne Nicolet et Perretta Alteram vero ex patre K8erasing et 8inchk8ck matre Lucia dicta est a Patrinus Nicolao Marsolet[1] et Margarita Couillard, uxor Domini Nicolet."

II.—FIRST CONNECTED SKETCH PUBLISHED OF THE LIFE AND EXPLORATION OF NICOLET.[2]

[Du Creux states that, in the last months of 1642, New France mourned for two men of no common character, who were snatched away from her; that one of them, who died first, of disease, was a member of the Society of Jesuits; and that the other, although a layman, was distinguished by singularly

---

[1] Nicolas Marsolet, connected, as an interpreter, with 3-Rivers, but mostly with Tadoussac and Quebec.

[2] Translated from Du Creux' Hist. of Canada (printed in Latin, in Paris, 1664), p. 358. That his account should not sooner have awakened the curiosity of students of American history is due to the fact previously mentioned, that not until the investigations of John Gilmary Shea, in 1853, were the "Ouinipigou" identified as the "Winnebagoes," and their having been visited by Nicolet established. It was this locating of the objective point of Nicolet's exploration on American soil that finally stimulated American writers to further research; though, to the present time, Canadian historians have taken the lead in investigations concerning the indomitable Frenchman.

meritorious acts towards the Indian tribes of Canada. He sketches briefly the career and character of Father Raymbault, the Jesuit, first referred to, who died at Quebec in the latter part of October. The second person alluded to was Nicolet. Of him he gives the following account:]

"He had spent twenty-five years in New France, and had always been a useful person. On his first arrival, by orders of those who presided over the French colony of Quebec, he spent two whole years among the Algonquins of the Island, for the purpose of learning their language, without any Frenchman as a companion, and in the midst of those hardships, which may be readily conceived, if we will reflect what it must be to pass severe winters in the woods, under a covering of cedar or birch bark; to have one's means of subsistence dependent upon hunting; to be perpetually hearing rude outcries; to be deprived of the pleasant society of one's own people; and to be constantly exposed, not only to derision and insulting words, but even to daily peril of life. There was a time, indeed, when he went without food for a whole week; and (what is really wonderful) he even spent seven weeks without having any thing to eat but a little bark. After this preliminary training[1] was completed, being sent with four hundred Algonquins to the Iroquois to treat of peace, he performed his mission successfully. Soon after, he went to the Nipissiriens, and spent seven years with them, as an adopted member of their tribe. He had

---

[1] *Tirocinium* is the *first campaign* of the young soldier; and so, generally, the first period of trial in any life of danger and hardship.—*Translator.*

his own small estate, wigwam, and household stuff, implements for hunting and fishing, and, no doubt, his own beaver skins, with the same right of trade as the rest; in a word, he was taken into their counsels; until, being recalled, by the rulers of the French colony, he was at the same time made a commissary and charged to perform the office of an interpreter.

"During this period, at the command of the same rulers, he had to make an excursion to certain maritime tribes, for the purpose of securing peace between them and the Hurons. The region where those peoples dwell is nearly three hundred leagues distant, toward the west, from the same Hurons; and after he had associated himself with seven ambassadors of these [*i. e.*, of the Hurons], having saluted on their route various small nations which they fell in with, and having propitiated them with gifts—lest, if they should omit this, they might be regarded as enemies, and assailed by all whom they met—when he was two days distant, he sent forward one of his own company to make known to the nation to which they were going, that a European ambassador was approaching with gifts, who, in behalf of the Hurons, desired to secure their friendship. The embassy was received with applause; young men were immediately sent to meet them, who were to carry the baggage and equipment of the Manitouriniou (or wonderful man), and escort him with honor. Nicolet was clad in a Chinese robe of silk, skillfully ornamented with birds and flowers of many colors; he carried in each hand a small pistol.[1] When he had discharged these,

---

[1] It may be interesting to the reader to know how pistols are

the more timid persons, **boys** and **women betook themselves to** flight, **to escape as quickly as** possible from a man who **(they said) carried the** thunder in both **his hands. But, the** rumor of his coming having **spread far and wide, the chiefs, with their followers,** assembled **directly to** the **number of four or five thousand** persons; **and, the matter having** been discussed and considered in **a** general council, **a** treaty was made in due form. **Afterwards each of the** chiefs gave a banquet after **their** fashion; **and at one of these,** strange **to say, a hundred and twenty** beavers **were** eaten.

" His object being accomplished, Nicolet returned to the Hurons, **and,** presently, **to** Three **Rivers,** and resumed both of his **former** functions, viz., as commissary **and interpreter,** being singularly beloved **by both the French and the** natives; specially **intent** upon this, **that, uniting his industry,** and the **very** great influence which he possessed **over the** savages, **with** the efforts of the fathers of the Society [Jesuits], he might bring as many as he could to the Church; until, **upon the** recall to France of Olivier, **who was** the chief commissary of Quebec, Nicolet, **on** account of **his** merits, **was** appointed in **his place.** But he was **not long** allowed **to** enjoy the **Christian** comfort he had so **greatly desired, viz.,** that at Quebec he might frequently attend **upon the** sacraments **as** his pious soul desired, and that he might **enjoy** the society of **those** with whom he could **converse upon** divine **things.**

---

described in the author's Latin: "Sclopos minores, exiis qui **tactâ** vel leviter rotulâ exploduntier."—*Translator.*

"On the last day of October, having embarked upon a pinnace at the seventh hour of the afternoon (as we French reckon the hours), i. e., just as the shades of evening were falling, hastening, as I have said, to Three Rivers upon so pious an errand, scarcely had he arrived in sight of Sillery, when, the north wind blowing more fiercely, and increasing the violence of the storm which had commenced before Nicolet started,[1] the pinnace was whirled around two or three times, filled with water from all directions, and finally was swallowed up by the waves. Some of those on board escaped, among them Savigny, the owner of the pinnace; and Nicolet, in that time of extreme peril, addressing him calmly said: "Savigny, since you know how to swim, by all means consult your own safety; I, who have no such skill, am going to God; I recommend my wife and daughter to your kindness." In the midst of this conversation, a wave separated them; Nicolet was drowned; Savigny, who, from horror and the darkness of the night, did not know where he was, was torn by the violence of the waves from the boat, to which he had clung for some time; then he struggled for a while, in swimming, with the hostile force of the changing waves; until, at last, his strength failing, and his courage almost forsaking him, he made a vow to God (but what it was is not related); then, striking the bottom of the stream with his foot,

---

[1] "Boreâ flaute pertinaciùs, fœdamque tempestatem, quam exciere gam ceperat, glomerante." Literally, perhaps, "the north wind blowing more persistently. and gathering into a mass the dark storm which it had already begun to collect."—*Translator.*

he reached the bank[1] at that spot, and, forcing his way with difficulty through the edge of the stream, already frozen, he crept, half dead, to the humble abode of the fathers. Restoratives were immediately applied, such as were at hand, especially fire, which was most needed; but, as the cold weather and the water had almost destroyed the natural warmth, he could only manifest his thoughts for some time by motions and not by speech, and so kept the minds of the anxious fathers in doubt of his meaning; until, recovering his speech, he explained what had happened with a strong expression of Nicolet's Christian courage.

"The prisoner for whose sake Nicolet had exposed himself to this deadly peril, twelve days afterwards reached Sillery, and soon after Quebec—having been rescued from the cruelty of the Algonquins by Rupæus, who was in command at Three Rivers, in pursuance of letters from Montmagny, on payment, no doubt, of a ransom. He was already disfigured with wounds, great numbers of which these most savage men had inflicted upon him with careful ingenuity, one after another, according to their custom; but in proportion to the barbarity which he had experienced at Three Rivers was the kindness which he afterwards met with at Quebec, where he was treated by the monks of the hospital in such a manner that he was healed within about twenty days, and was able to return to his own people. . . .

"This, moreover, was not the first occasion on which

[1] The word "littus" here is properly used, not of the dry land, but of the sloping land under the water, near the edge of the river.—*Translator.*

Nicolet had encountered peril of his life for the safety of savages. He had frequently done the very same thing before, says the French writer; and to those with whom he associated he left proofs of his virtues by such deeds as could hardly be expected of a man entangled in the bonds of marriage; they were indeed eminent, and rose to the height of apostolic perfection; and, therefore, was the loss of so great a man the more grievous. Certain it is that the savages themselves, as soon as they heard what had befallen him, surrounded the bank of the great river in crowds, to see whether they could render any aid. When all hope of that was gone, they did what alone remained in their power, by incredible manifestations of grief and lamentation at the sad fate of the man who had deserved so well of them."

INDEX.

Alizon, M., 95, 100.
Algonquins, viii, 17, 36, 42, 60, 62, 69, 76, 77, 87.
Algonquins of the Isles des Allumettes, 18, 28, 29, 46.
Allouez, Father Claudius, 64, 67, 69.
Amikoüai, " Nation of the Beaver," 50, 51, 54.
An account of the French settlements in North America (1746), **cited,** 32.
A8eatsi8nenrrhouon (Aweatsiwaerrhonon), Huron name for the Winnebagoes, 45, 46, 60.
Assiniboins, not visited by Nicolet, 71.
Atchiligoüan, an Algonquin nation, 50.
Bay des Puants (Baie des Puants). **See Green Bay.**
Beaver **Nation, 45, 48, 50, 51, 54, 63.**
Bonhomme, **Nicholas, 98.**
Brébeuf, John **de,** 20, 24, **41,** 46, 100.
Buteux, Father James, 78, 80, 93, 94, **95, 96, 97.**
Cabot, John, viii, ix.
Cabot, Sebastian, ix.
Caens, the, 21.
Capitanal, a Montagnais chief, 93.
Cartier, James, 11, 12, 13, 14, 15.
Champlain's **Map** of **1632,** referred to, 31, 35, 36, 38, 51, 52, 53, 54, 62, 64, 66, 70.
Champlain, Samuel, makes, in 1603, a survey of the St. Lawrence, 16; in 1608, founds Quebec, 17; attacks the Iroquois, in 1609, *ib.;* returns, in 1610, to France, 18; in 1611 again reaches the St. Lawrence, *ib.;* soon sails back to France, *ib.;* in 1613, once more reaches the St. Lawrence, *ib.;* explores the Ottawa to the Isle des Allumettes, *ib.;* embarks for **France,** *ib.;* in 1615, again sails for New France, 19; visits the Hurons, *ib.;* attacks, with those Indians, the Iroquois, *ib.;* returns to Quebec, 20; a new government for New France, 21; Champlain one of the Hundred Associates, 22; he defends Quebec against the English, 23;

next year he surrenders the town, *ib.;* taken a prisoner to England, 24; in 1633, resumes command in New France, *ib.;* resolves to explore the west, *ib.;* in 1634, sends Nicolet to the Winnebagoes, 39; death of Champlain, 75.

Champlain's *Voyages* of 1613, cited, 36; *Voyages* of 1632, cited, 36, 38, 51, 52, 64, 66, 73.

Charlevoix' *Carte des Lacs du Canada*, referred to, 57; also, his *Nouvelle France, ib.*

Chauvin, a captain of the French marine, 15.

Cheveux Relevés (Standing Hair—Ottawas), 52, 53, 54, 73.

Chippewas, 38, 53, 54, 55, 90, 91.

Cioux. See Sioux.

Columbus, Christopher, viii.

Company of New France, 21.

Copper and copper mine early known to the Indians, 36.

Cortereal, Gaspar, ix.

Couillard, Guillaume, 82.

Couillard, Marguerite, 81, 84, 94, 98, 99, 100.

Coureurs de bois, 41.

Cresse, M., 90.

Crevier, François, 97.

Daniel, Antoine, a Jesuit priest, 41, 80.

Dakotas (Dacotahs.—See Sioux), viii, 62, 71.

Davost, a Jesuit, 41.

De Caen, Émery, 20, 24, 32.

De Caen, William, 20.

De Champfleur, François, 98.

De Chasteaufort, Bras-de-fer, 75.

De Courtemanche, Augustin le, 84.

De Gand, François Derré, 82.

Delaplace, Jacques, 94.

De Laubin, M., 90.

De la Roche, the Marquis, 15.

De la Roque, John Francis, see Lord of Roberval.

De Malapart, M., 95.

De Maupertius, M, 93.

De Repentigny, Jean-Baptiste l'Gardeur, 84.

Des Roches, M., 85, 88.

Des Gens Puants (Des Gens Puans—Des Puants—Des Puans). See Winnebagoes.

Du Creux' *Hist. of Canada* (*Historia Canadensis*), cited, 29, 60, 100, *et seq.*
Du Creux' Map of 1660, referred to, 51, 53, 55, **73**
Enitajghe, **Iroquois** name for Green Bay, 56.
Estinghicks, **Iroquois name** of the Chippewas, 52.
Fire Nations (**Les Gens de Feu**). See Mascoutins.
Foster's *Mississippi Valley*, cited, **59**.
Fox River of Green Bay, 61, 64, 66, 67, 68, **70**.
Fox Indians (Outagamis—Les Renards—Musquakies), 64, 65, 66.
Fur-trade, the, 22.
Ferland's *Cours d' Histoire du Canada*, cited, 27, 82, 89; also, his *Notes sur les Registres de Notre-Dame de Québec*, 27, 82, 85.
Gens de Mer (Gens de Eaux de Mer). See Winnebagoes.
Godefroy, Jean, 94, 95.
Godefroy, Louis, **95**.
Godefroy, Thomas, 96.
Gravier's *Découvertes et Établissement de Cavalier de la Salle*, cited, 82; his *Map by Joliet*, referred to, 55, 59.
Green Bay, 56, 60, 62, 69, 70.
Guitet, a notary, records of, 27, 82.
Hébert, **Guilleme 82**.
Hébert, Guillamet, 82.
Hertel, Jacques, 99.
Hertel, François, 99.
Horoji (Hochungara—Winnebagoes), 60.
Huboust, Guillaume, 82.
Hundred Associates (Hundred Partners), **21, 22,** 23, 24, 25, 31, 39, 42, 76, **82**.
Hurons, 17, 19, 21, 23, 36, **42,** 43, 47, 48, 49, 51, 62, 63, 69, 76, 77, 102, 103
Illinois (Indians), **70**.
Iroquois, **17, 18,** 20, **29, 38, 44, 51, 76**.
Jesuits, the, **68, 80, 85**.
Jesuit Relations, the, **27**.
Jesuit Relations, cited: 1633—93; 1635—44, **46,** 93; 1636—30, **45, 60,** 77, 78, 79, **80**; 1637—78, 80, 81; 1638—80; 1639—60; **1640—38,** 45, **48,** 50, **51, 53,** 56, 57, 62, 67, **68, 69,** 70, 72, 73; 1641—82; 1642—53; 1643—26, 27, 28, 30, 47, 48, 49, 58, 60, 62, 72, 74, 78, 83, 84, 85, 86, 87, 88; 1648—38, 53; 1654—38, 69; 1656—62, 70; 1670—64, 67, 69; 1671—53, 56, 64.
Joliet, Jean, 96.

Joliet, Louis, 68, 69, 96.
Joques, Father Isaac, 91, 97.
Juchereau, Noël, 82.
Kaukauna, town of, 65.
Kirk, David, 23.
Kickapoos (Kikabou, Kikapou, Quicapou, Kickapoux, Kickapous, Kikapoux, Quicpouz), 67.
La Baye (La Baye des Eaux Puantes—La Grande Baie—La Baye des Puans—Lay Baye des Puants). See Green Bay.
Lake Michigan (Lake of the Illinois—Lake St. Joseph—Lake Dauphin—Lac des Illinois—Lac Missihiganin—Magnus Lacus Algonquinorum). 55, 56, 66, 69, 70, 72.
Lake Superior, 54.
Lake Winnebago (Lake of the Puants—Lake St. Francis), 62, 65.
La Marchand, Jeanne, 99.
La Mélée, Christopher Crevier, Sieur de, 97.
La Mer, Marguerite, 27.
La Mer, Maria, 27.
La Nation des Puans (La Nation des Puants). See Winnebagoes.
La Nouë, Annie de, 24, 41.
La Porte, Pierre de, 82.
La Vallée, Claude, 99.
Lavidiere's *Reprint of Champlain's Works*, referred to, 36.
Le Caron, Father Joseph, 19, 20.
Les Folles Avoine. See Menomonees.
Le Jeune, Paul, 24, 41, 80.
Le Neuf, family of, 94.
Le Neuf, Maria 94, 95, 98.
Le Tardif, Olivier, 82, 83, 84, 103.
Lord of Roberval, 14, 15.
Lippincott's *Gazetteer*, cited, 33.
Mackinaw, Straits of, 55.
Macard, Nicolas, 84, 100.
Manitoulin Islands, 50, 51.
Mantoue (Mantoucouee—Makoueoue), tribe of, 56.
Marguerie, François, 95, 99.
Marguerie, Maria, 99.
Margry, Pierre, in *Journal Général de l'Instruction Publique*, 29, 72, 84.
Marquette, Father James, 68, 69.
Marsolet, Nicolas, 84, 100.
Mascoutins (Macoutins—Mascoutens—Maskoutens — Maskouteins—

INDEX. 111

Musquetens—Machkoutens—Maskoutench—Machkoutenck—Les Gens de Feu—The Fire Nation—Assistagueronons—Assistaehronons), 51, 52, 63, 64, 65, 66, 67, 68, 69, 70.

Masse, the Jesuit, 41.

Menomonees (Maromine—Malhominies—Les **Folles Avoine**), 57, 58.

Miamis, 67.

Michigan, **signification** of the word, 65.

Mississippi, meaning of the word, 67.

Montmagnais, 36, 41.

Montmagny, M. de, 70, 75, 76, 77, **105**.

Nantoue. See Mantoue.

Nation des Puans (Nation des **Puants—Nation** of Stinkards). See Winnebagoes.

Nation du Castor (Nation of **Beavers**). See Beaver Nation.

Nation of the Sault. See Chippewas.

Nenascoumat, an Indian chief, 95.

Neutral Nation, 51, 61, 65.

Nez Percés (Naiz percez). See Beaver Nation.

Nicolet, Gilles, 88, 89.

Nicolet, **John, arrives** in New France, 26; sent by Champlain, **in 1618, to the Algonquins of Isle des** Allumettes, 28; goes on a mission of peace to **the Iroquois, 29;** takes up his residence with the Nipissings, *ib.;* recalled by the government to Quebec, 30; employed as interpreter, *ib.;* **Champlain resolves to send him on a** western exploration, 33; Nicolet had **heard of the Winnebagoes,** 39; prepares, in June, 1634, to visit this **and** other nations, 40; starts upon his journey, 42; **why it must have been** in 1634 **that** Nicolet made his westward exploration, *ib., et seq.;* travels **up the** Ottawa to the Isle des Allumettes, **46;** goes hence to the **Huron villages,** 47; object of his mission there, **48; starts** for the Winnebagoes, **49; reaches Sault Sainte** Marie, 51; did he see Lake Superior? **54; discovers Lake** Michigan, 55; arrives at the Menomonee river, 56; **ascends** Green Bay to the homes of the Winnebagoes, 60; has a great feast with **the Indians,** 62; goes up **Fox** river to the Mascoutins, 63; visits the Illinois tribe, 71; returns to the Winnebagoes, *ib.;* Nicolet's homeward trip in 1635—he **calls** upon **the Pottawattamies,** 72; stops **at** the Great Manatoulin to see a band of **Ottawas, 73; reaches** the St. Lawrence in safety, 74; settles at Three Rivers as interpreter, 77; his kindness to the Indians, 78; has a narrow escape from drowning, 81; helps defend Three Rivers from an Iroquois attack, *ib.;* his marriage, *ib.;* goes to

Quebec, 82; becomes General Commissary of the Hundred Partners, *ib.*; embarks for Three Rivers, 83; his death, 84; Frenchmen and Indians alike mourn his fate, 87; his memory perpetuated, 89; his energetic character, 90; mention of him in the parish register of Three Rivers, 93, *et seq.*; first connected sketch published of his life and exploration, 100, *et seq.*

Nicolet, Madame, 95, 96.
Nicolet, Pierre, 89.
Nicolet, Thomas, 27.
Nipissings (Nipisiriniens), 29, 30, 31, 43, 47.
Noquets, 56.
O'Callaghan's *Doc. Hist. of New York*, referred to, 36; his *N. Y. Col. Doc.*, cited, 51.
Ojibwas. See Chippewas.
Ottawas, 50, 52, 54, 65, 66, 73.
"Ounipeg," signification of, 38.
Ounipigou. See Winnegagoes.
Oumalouminck (Oumacminiees). See Menomonees.
Otchagras (Ochungarand). See Winnebagoes.
Otchipwes. See Chippewas.
Ouasouarim, 50.
Oumisagai, 51, 54.
Outchougai, 50.
Outaouan. See Ottawas.
Parkman's *Jesuits in North America*, cited, 41, 43, 46, 80; also, his *La Salle and the Discovery of the Great West*, 38, 58; and his *Pioneers of France in the New World*, 52.
"People of the Falls." See Chippewas.
"People of the Sea." See Winnebagoes.
Perot, Nicolas, 84.
Petun Nation, 51, 52.
Pijart, Claudius, 96.
Poncet, Josephus, 98, 99.
Pontgrave, merchant, 15.
Pottawattamies, 71.
Quentin, Father Claude, 77, 78, 79, 93.
Racine, Claude, 82.
Racine, Etienne, 82.
Raratwaus. See Chippewas.
Raymbault, Father Charles, 83, 86, 91, 97, 101.
Richelieu, Cardinal, 21.

INDEX. 113

River des Puans (River of the Puants—River St. Francis). See Fox river.
Rollet, Marie, **82**.
Roquai. See Noquets.
Sacs (Sauks—**Saukis—Sakys**), 64.
Sagard's *Historie du Canada*, cited, 38.
Sauteurs (Stiagigroone). See Chippewas.
Sault de Sainte Marie, 51.
Sault Sainte Marie, town of, 54, 72, 97.
Savigny (Chavigny), 83, 84, 85, 86, 104.
Schoolcraft's *Thirty Years with the Indian Tribes*, cited, 59.
"Sea-Tribe." See Winnebagoes.
Shea's *Catholic Missions*, cited, 53; also, his *Discovery and Exploration of the Mississippi Valley*, 38, 45, 59, 63, 100; and his *Hennepin*, 67.
Shea, John Gilmary, in *Wis. Hist. Soc. Coll.*, 73.
Sillery, mission of, founded, 76.
Sioux (Dacotas), 37, 62, 71.
St. Croix Fort, established, **32**.
Smith's *History of* **Wisconsin**, cited, 27, 38, 73.
Standing Hair, the. **See Ottawas**.
Sulte, Benjamin, in *L'Opinion* **Publique**, 68, 90.
Sulte's *Chronique Trifluvienne*, cited, 31; also, his *Mélanges de Historie et de Littérature*, 43, 84, 89.
"The Men of the Shallow Cataract." See Chippewas.
Three Rivers, town of, 31, 32, 33, 42, 45, 74, 77, 78, 79, 82, **83, 86**, 103.
Three Rivers, parish church register of, 44, 45, 93, *et seq*.
Tobacco **Nation**. See Petun Nation.
Verrazzano, John, ix.
Winnebagoes, **viii**, 37, 38, **39, 42**, 43, 44, 45, 46, 48, **49, 50, 57, 58, 60**, 61, 62, 63, 64, 71, **72, 74**, 77.
Wisconsin, derivation of the word, **59**
Wisconsin river, 59, **61, 68**.
Woolf river, 35, 66.
Woodman, Cyrus, 27.

OCT. 1881.

HISTORICAL AND MISCELLANEOUS
PUBLICATIONS OF
ROBERT CLARKE & CO.
CINCINNATI, O.

ALZOG (John, D. D.) A Manual of Universal Church History. Translated by Rev. T. J. Pabisch and Rev. T. S. Byrne. 3 vols. 8vo. 15 00

ANDERSON (E. L.) Six Weeks in Norway. 18mo. 1 00

ANDRE (Major) The Cow Chace; an Heroick Poem. 8vo. Paper. 75

ANTRIM (J.) The History of Champaign and Logan Counties, Ohio, from their First Settlement. 12mo. 1 50

BALLARD (Julia P.) Insect Lives; or, Born in Prison. Illustrated. Sq. 12mo. 1 00

BELL (Thomas J.) History of the Cincinnati Water Works. Plates. 8vo. 75

BENNER (S.) Prophecies of Future Ups and Downs in Prices: what years to make Money in Pig Iron, Hogs, Corn, and Provisions. 2d ed. 24mo. 1 00

BIBLE IN THE PUBLIC SCHOOLS. Records, Arguments, etc., in the Case of Minor vs. Board of Education of Cincinnati. 8vo. 2 00

    Arguments in Favor of the Use of the Bible. Separate. Paper. 50

    Arguments Against the Use of the Bible. Separate. Paper. 50

BIDDLE (Horace P.) Elements of Knowledge. 12mo. 1 00

BIDDLE (Horace P.) Prose Miscellanies. 12mo. 1 00

BINKERD (A. D.) The Mammoth Cave of Kentucky. Paper. 8vo. 50

BOUQUET (H.) The Expedition of, against the Ohio Indians in 1764, etc. With Preface by Francis Parkman, Jr. 8vo. $3 00. Large Paper. 6 00

BOYLAND (G. H., M. D.) Six Months Under the Red Cross with the French Army in the Franco-Prussian War. 12mo. 1 50

BRUNNER (A. A.) Elementary and Pronouncing French Reader. 18mo. 60

BRUNNER (A. A.) The Gender of French Verbs Simplified. 18mo. 25

BURT (Rev. N. C., D. D.) The Far East; or, Letters from Egypt, Palestine, etc. 12mo. 1 75

BUTTERFIELD (C. W.) The Washington-Crawford Letters; being the Correspondence between George Washington and William Crawford, concerning Western Lands. 8vo. 1 00

BUTTERFIELD (C W.) The Discovery of the Northwest in 1634, by John Nicolet, with a Sketch of his Life. 12mo. 1 00

CLARK (Col. George Rogers) Sketches of his Campaign in the Illinois in 1778-9. With an Introduction by Hon. Henry Pirtle, and an Appendix. 8vo. $2 00. Large paper. 4 00

COFFIN (Levi) The Reminiscences of Levi Coffin, the Reputed President of the Underground Railroad. A Brief History of the Labors of a Lifetime in behalf of the Slave. With Stories of Fugitive Slaves, etc., etc. 12mo. 2 00

CONSTITUTION OF THE UNITED STATES, ETC. The Declaration of Independence, July 4, 1776, the Articles of Confederation, July 9, 1778; the Constitution of the United States, September 17, 1787; the Fifteen Amendments to the Constitution, and Index; Washington's Farewell Address, September 7, 1796. 8vo. Paper. 25

CRAIG (N. B.) The Olden Time. A Monthly Publication, devoted to the Preservation of Documents of Early History, etc. Originally Published at Pittsburg, in 1846-47. 2 vols. 8vo. 10 00

DRAKE (D.) Pioneer Life in Kentucky. Edited, with Notes and a Biographical Sketch, by his Son, Hon. Chas. D. Drake. 8vo. $3 00. Large paper. 6 00

DUBREUIL (A.) Vineyard Culture Improved and Cheapened. Edited by Dr. J. A. Warder. 12mo. 2 00

ELLARD (Virginia G.) Grandma's Christmas Day. Illus. Sq. 12mo. 1 00

FAMILY EXPENSE BOOK. A Printed Account Book, with appropriate Columns and Headings, for keeping a Complete Record of Family Expenses. 12mo. 50

FINLEY (I. J.) and PUTNAM (R.) Pioneer Record and Reminiscences of the Early Settlers and Settlement of Ross County, Ohio. 8vo. 2 50

FLETCHER (WM. B., M. D.) Cholera: its Characteristics, History, Treatment, etc. 8vo. Paper. 1 00

FORCE (M. F.) Essays: Pre-Historic Man—Darwinism and Deity —The Mound Builders. 8vo. Paper. 75

Force (M. F.) Some Early Notices of the Indians of Ohio. To What Race did the Mound Builders belong. 8vo. Paper. 50

Freeman (Ellen.) Manual of the French Verb, to accompany every French Course. 16mo. Paper. 25

Gallagher (Wm. D.) Miami Woods, A Golden Wedding, and other Poems. 12mo. 2 00

Giauque (F.) The Election Laws of the United States: with Notes of Decisions, etc. 8vo. Paper, 75c.; cloth, 1 00

Grimke (F.) Considerations on the Nature and Tendency of Free Institutions. 8vo. 2 50

Griswold (W.) Kansas: her Resources and Developments; or, the Kansas Pilot. 8vo. Paper. 50

Groesbeck (W. S.) Gold and Silver. Address delivered before the American Bankers' Association, in New York, September 13, 1878. 8vo. Paper. 25

Hall (James.) Legends of the West. Sketches illustrative of the Habits, Occupations, Privations, Adventures, and Sports of the Pioneers of the West. 12mo. 2 00

Hall (James.) Romance of Western History; or, Sketches of History, Life, and Manners in the West. 12mo. 2 00

Hanover (M. D.) A Practical Treatise on the Law of Horses, embracing the Law of Bargain, Sale, and Warranty of Horses and other Live Stock; the Rule as to Unsoundness and Vice, and the Responsibility of the Proprietors of Livery, Auction, and Sale Stables, Inn-Keepers, Veterinary Surgeons, and Farriers, Carriers, etc. 8vo. 4 00

Hart (J. M.) A Syllabus of Anglo-Saxon Literature. 8vo. Paper. 50

Hassaurek (F.) The Secret of the Andes. A Romance. 12mo. 1 50
The Same, in German. 8vo. Paper, 50c.; cloth. 1 00

Hassaurek (F.) Four Years Among Spanish Americans. Third Edition. 12mo. 1 50

Hatch (Col. W. S.) A Chapter in the History of the War of 1812, in the Northwest, embracing the Surrender of the Northwestern Army and Fort, at Detroit, August 16, 1813, etc. 18mo. **1 25**

Hayes (Rutherford B.) The Life, Public Services, and **Select** Speeches of. Edited by J. Q. Howard. 12mo. Paper, 75c.; cloth, 1 25

Hazen (Gen. W. B.) Our Barren Lands. The Interior of the United States, West of the One-Hundredth Meridian, and East of the Sierra Nevada. 8vo. Paper. 50

HENSHALL. (Dr. James A.) Book of the Black Bass: comprising its complete Scientific and Life History, together with a Practical Treatise on Agling and Fly Fishing, and a full description of Tools, Tackle, and Implements. Illustrated. 12mo. 3 00

HORTON (S. Dana.) Silver and Gold, and their Relation to the Problem of Resumption. 8vo. 1 50

HORTON (S. Dana.) The Monetary Situation. 8vo. Paper. 50

HOUSEKEEPING IN THE BLUE GRASS. A New and Practical Cook Book. By Ladies of the Presbyterian Church, Paris, Ky. 12mo. 12th thousand. 1 50

HOWE (H.) Historical Collections of Ohio. Containing a Collection of the most Interesting Facts, Traditions, Biographical Sketches, Anecdotes, etc., relating to its Local and General History. 8vo. 6 00

HUNT (W. E.) Historical Collections of Coshocton County, Ohio. 8vo. 3 00

HUSTON (R. G.) Journey in Honduras, and Jottings by the Way. Inter-Oceanic Railway. 8vo. Paper. 50

JACKSON (John D., M. D.) The Black Arts in Medicine, with an Anniversary Address. Edited by Dr. L. S. McMurtry. 12mo. 1 00

JASPER (T.) The Birds of North America. Colored Plates, drawn from Nature, with Descriptive and Scientific Letterpress. In 40 parts, $1 00 each; or, 2 vols. Royal 4to. Half morocco, $50 00; Full morocco, 60 00

JORDAN (D. M.) Rosemary Leaves. A Collection of Poems. 18mo. 1 50

KELLER (M. J.) Elementary Perspective, explained and applied to Familiar Objects. Illustrated. 12mo. 1 00

KING (John.) A Commentary on the Law and True Construction of the Federal Constitution. 8vo. 2 50

KING (M.) Pocket-Book of Cincinnati. 24mo. 15

KLIPPART (J. H.) The Principles and Practice of Land Drainage. Illustrated. 12mo. 1 75

LAW (J.) Colonial History of Vincennes, Indiana, under the French, British, and American Governments. 12mo. 1 00

LLOYD (J. U.) The Chemistry of Medicines. Illus. 12mo. Cloth, $2 75; sheep, 3 25

LONGWORTH (N.) Electra. Translated from the Greek of Sophocles. 12mo. 1 50

McBRIDE (J.) Pioneer Biography · Sketches of the Lives of some of the Early Settlers of Butler County, Ohio. 2 vols. 8vo. $6 50. Large paper. Imp. 8vo. 13 00

McLaughlin (M. Louise.) China Painting. A Practical Manual for the Use of Amateurs in the Decoration of Hard Porcelain. Sq. 12mo. Boards. 75

McLaughlin (M. Louise.) Pottery Decoration: being a Practical Manual of Underglaze Painting, including Complete Detail of the author's Mode of Painting Enameled Faience. Sq. 12mo. Bds. 1 00

MacLean (J. P.) The Mound Builders, and an Investigation into the Archæology of Butler County, Ohio. Illus. 12mo. 1 50

MacLean (J P) A Manual of the Antiquity of Man. Illustrated. 12mo. 1 00

MacLean (J. P.) Mastodon, Mammoth, and Man. Illustrated. 12mo. 60

Mansfield (E. D.) Personal Memories, Social, Political, and Literary. 1803–43. 12mo. 2 00

Manypenny (G. W.) **Our** Indian Wards: **A** History and Discussion of the Indian **Question.** 8vo. 3 00

Matthews (Stanley.) **A** Summary of the Law of Partnership. For the Use of Business Men. 12mo. 1 25

May (Col. J.) Journal and Letters of, relative to Two Journeys to the Ohio Country, 1788 and 1779. 8vo. 2 00

Mettenheimer (H. J.) Safety Book-keeping; being a Complete Exposition of Book-keepers' Frauds. 12mo. 1 00

Minor (T. C., M. D.) Child-Bed Fever. Erysipelas and Puerperal Fever, with a Short Account of both Diseases. 8vo. 2 00

Minor (T. C., M. **D.**) Scarlatina Statistics of the United States. **8vo.** Paper. 50

Montana Historical Society. Contributions. Vol. I, 8vo. 3 00

Morgan (Appleton.) The Shakspearean Myth; or, William Shakspeare and Circumstantial Evidence. 12mo. 2 00

Name and Address Book. A Blank Book, with printed Headings and Alphabetical Marginal Index, for Recording the Names and Addresses of Professional, Commercial, and Family Correspondents. 8vo. 1 00

Nash (Simeon.) **Crime and** the Family. 12mo. 1 25

Nerinckx (Rev. Charles.) Life of, with Early Catholic Missions in Kentucky; the Society of Jesus; the Sisterhood of Loretto, etc. By Rev. C. P. Maes. 8vo. 2 50

Nichols (G. W.) The Cincinnati Organ; with a Brief Description of the Cincinnati Music Hall. 12mo. Paper. 25

Ohio Valley Historical Miscellanies. I. Memorandums of a Tour Made by Josiah Espy, in the States of Ohio and Kentucky, and Indiana Territory, in 1805. II. Two Western Campaigns in the War of 1812–13: 1. Expedition of Capt. H. Brush, with Supplies for General Hull. 2. Expedition of Gov. Meigs, for the relief of Fort Meigs. By Samuel Williams. III. The Leatherwood God: an account of the Appearance and Pretensions of J. C. Dylks in Eastern Ohio, in 1828. By R. H. Taneyhill. 1 vol. 8vo. $2 50. Large paper, 5 00

ONCE A YEAR; or, The Doctor's Puzzle. By E. B. S. 16mo. 1 00

PHISTERER (Captain Frederick.) The National Guardsman: on Guard and Kindred Duties. 24mo. Leather. 75

PHYSICIAN'S POCKET CASE RECORD PRESCRIPTION BOOK. 35

PHYSICIAN'S GENERAL LEDGER. Half Russia. 4 00

PIATT (John J.) Penciled Fly-Leaves. A Book of Essays in Town and Country. Sq. 16mo. 1 00

POOLE (W. F.) Anti-Slavery Opinions before 1800. An Essay. 8vo. Paper, 75c.; cloth, 1 25

PRACTICAL RECEIPTS OF EXPERIENCED HOUSE-KEEPERS. By the ladies of the Seventh Presbyterian Church, Cin. 12mo. 1 25

PRENTICE (Geo. D.) Poems of, collected and edited, with Biographical Sketch, by John J. Piatt. 12mo. 2 00

QUICK (R. H.) Essays on Educational Reformers. 12mo. 1 50

RANCK (G. W.) History of Lexington, Kentucky. Its Early Annals and Recent Progress, etc. 8vo. 4 00

REEMELIN (C.) The Wine-Maker's Manual. A Plain, Practical Guide to all the Operations for the Manufacture of Still and Sparkling Wines. 12mo. 1 25

REEMELIN (C.) A Treatise on Politics as a Science. 8vo. 1 50

REEMELIN (C.) A Critical Review of American Politics. 8vo. *In Press.*

RIVES (E., M. D.) A Chart of the Physiological Arrangement of Cranial Nerves. Printed in large type, on a sheet 28x15 inches. Folded, in cloth case. 50

ROBERT (Karl). Charcoal Drawing with out a Master. A Complete Treatise in Landscape Drawing in Charcoal, with Lessons and Studies after Allonge. Translated by E. H. Appleton. Illustrated. 8vo 1 00

ROY (George). Generalship; or, How I Managed my Husband. A tale. 18mo. Paper, 50c.; cloth, 1 00

ROY (George). The Art of Pleasing. A Lecture. 12mo. Paper. 25

ROY (George). The Old, Old Story. A Lecture. 12mo. Paper. 25

RUSSELL (A. P.). Thomas Corwin. A Sketch. 16mo. 1 00

RUSSELL (Wm.) Scientific Horseshoeing for the Different Diseases of the Feet. Illustrated. 8vo. 1 00

SAYLER (J. A.) American Form Book. A Collection of Legal and Business Forms, embracing Deeds, Mortgages, Leases, Bonds, Wills, Contracts, Bills of Exchange, Promissory Notes, Checks, Bills of Sale, Receipts, and other Legal Instruments, prepared in accordance with the Laws of the several States; with Instructions for drawing and executing the same. For Professional and Business Men. 8vo. 2 00

SHEETS (Mary R.) **My Three** Angels: Faith, **Hope**, and **Love**. With full-page illustrations by E. D. Grafton. 4to. Cloth. Gilt. 5 00

SKINNER (J. R.) The Source of Measures. **A Key to the Hebrew-**Egyptian Mystery in the Source of Measures, etc. 8vo. 5 00

SMITH (Col. JAMES). A Reprint of an Account of the Remarkable Occurrences in his Life and Travels, during his Captivity with the Indians in the years 1755, '56, '57, '58, and '59, etc. 8vo. $2 50. Large paper, 5 00

STANTON (H.) Jacob Brown **and** other Poems. 12mo. 1 50

ST. CLAIR PAPERS. A Collection of the Correspondence and other papers of General Arthur St. Clair, Governor of the Northwest Territory. Edited, with a Sketch of his Life and Public Services, by William Henry Smith. *In Press.*

STRAUCH (A.) Spring Grove Cemetery, Cincinnati: its History and improvements, with Observations on Ancient and modern Places of Sepulture. The text beautifully printed with ornamental, colored borders, and photographic illustrations. 4to. Cloth. Gilt. 15 00

An 8vo edition, without border and illustrations. 2 00

STUDER (J. H.) Columbus, Ohio: its History, Resources, and Pro**gress,** from its Settlement to the Present Time. 12mo. 2 00

TANEYHILL (R. H.) The Leatherwood God: an account of the Appearance and Pretensions of Joseph C. Dylks in Eastern Ohio, in 1826. 12mo. Paper. 30

TEN BROOK (A.) **American** State Universities. Their Origin and Progress. A History of the Congressional University Land Grants. A particular account of the Rise and Development of the University of Michigan, and Hints toward the future of the American University System. 8vo. 2 00

TILDEN (Louise W.) Karl and Gretchen's Christmas. Illustrated. Square 12mo. 75

TILDEN (Louise **W.**) Poem, Hymn, and Mission Band Exercises. Written and arranged for the use of Foreign Missionary Societies and Mission Bands. Square 12mo. Paper. 25

TRENT (Capt. Wm.) Journal of, from Logstown to Pickawillany, in 1752. Edited **by** A. T. Goodman. 8vo. 2 50

Historical and Miscellaneous Publications.

TRIPLER (C. S., M.D.) and BLACKMAN (G. C., M.D.) Handbook for the Military Surgeon. 12mo. 1 00

TYLER DAVIDSON FOUNTAIN. History and Description of the Tyler Davidson Fountain, Donated to the City of Cincinnati, by Henry Probasco. 18mo. Paper. 25

VAGO (A. L.) Instructions in the art of Modeling in Clay. With an Appendix on Modeling in Foliage, etc., for Pottery and Architectural Decorations, by Benn Pitman, of Cincinnati School of Design. Illustrated. Square 12mo. 1 00

VAN HORNE (T. B.) The History of the Army of the Cumberland; its Organization, Campaigns, and Battles. *Library Edition.* 2 vols. With Atlas of 22 maps, compiled by Edward Ruger. 8vo. Cloth, $8 00; Sheep, $10 00; Half Morocco, $12 00. *Popular Edition.* Containing the same Text as the Library Edition, but only one map. 2 vols. 8vo. Cloth. 5 00

VENABLE (W. H.) June on the Miami, and other Poems. Second edition. 18mo. 1 50

VOORHEES (D. W.) Speeches of, embracing his most prominent Forensic, Political, Occasional, and Literary Addresses. Compiled by his son, C. S. Voorhees, with a Biographical Sketch and Portrait. 8vo. 5 00

WALKER (C. M.) History of Athens County, Ohio, and incidentally of the Ohio Land Company, and the First Settlement of the State at Marietta, etc. 8vo. $6 00. Large Paper. 2 vols. $12 00. Popular Edition. 4 00

WALTON (G. E.) Hygiene and Education of Infants; or, How to take care of Babies. 24mo. Paper. 25

WARD (Durbin). American Coinage and Currency. An Essay read before the Social Science Congress, at Cincinnati, May 22, 1878. 8vo. Paper. 10

WEBB (F.) and JOHNSTON (M. C.) An Improved Tally-Book, for the use of Lumber Dealers. 18mo. 50

WHITTAKER (J. T., M. D.) Physiology; Preliminary Lectures. Illustrated. 12mo. 1 75

WILLIAMS (A. D., M. D.) Diseases of the Ear, including Necessary Anatomy of the Organ. 8vo. 3 50

YOUNG (A.) History of Wayne County, Indiana, from its First Settlement to the Present Time. 8vo. 2 00

www.ingramcontent.com/pod-product-compliance
Lightning Source LLC
Chambersburg PA
CBHW022141160426
43197CB00009B/1380